ABOUT THE AUTHOR

Dr Richard G. Lewis FCIM is one of the Internet's leading consultants and authors, specializing in e-commerce, buyer psychology and marketing. Over the last twelve years he has designed or developed over seventy e-commerce projects, many of which are now leaders in their market sector.

Richard has degrees in both business and computing, and holds a doctorate in e-commerce. He has over twenty five years experience of managing small businesses in the marketing, retail, service, and e-commerce sectors.

Richard has also written numerous research papers and books, including the bestseller, "The Small Business Guide to the Internet" (1999).

He is currently designing and developing websites for various high profile clients in the retail and Internet solutions sectors. Richard is available for consultancy work by contacting him through his website www.riskeliminator.com

Fortune Cookie

The Final Secret
(The ONLY Way Left To Make
$ERIOUS MONEY Online!)

Dr. Richard G. Lewis

Riana Publishing
International

Published by *Riana Publishing*
A division of The Riana Group

A catalogue record of this book is
available from the British Library.

ISBN 13 978-0-9558640-1-8

Earnings and Income Disclaimer

Every effort has been made by the author to accurately represent the potential of income from using the advice in this book. However, the author offers no guarantee, whether expressed or implied, that you will earn any money using the products, publications, documents, services, techniques, advice and/or ideas suggested in this book. The earning potential is entirely dependent on the person or organization using the author's products, services, publications, documents, advice, ideas and/or techniques.

This is not a "Get Rich Quick" scheme. The author has no way of knowing how well you will do, as the author does not know you, your background, your work ethic, your level of commitment, your financial standing or your business skills. The author DOES NOT guarantee, imply or predict that you will get rich, that you will do as well as others or that you will earn any money at all.

Your level of success in attaining the results claimed or promised in the author's materials may vary. Your success depends totally on the time and effort you devote to the program, ideas, suggestions and techniques mentioned, your knowledge, wisdom, experience, intuition, skills, efforts, behavior, education, expertise, level of desire and individual capacity. Since these factors and circumstances vary according to individuals, the author cannot guarantee your success, performance or income level.

The author disclaims any and all liability, both tangible and intangible, for loss or risk incurred as a consequence of the use and application, either directly or indirectly, of any advice, information, methods and techniques presented by the author through any and all mediums - including, but not limited to, oral, visual and written direction.

The information included in this book and any accompanying literature and products, with regard to various business or marketing methods, is for information purposes only.

DEDICATIONS

This book is dedicated to the memory of my father, Colin.

Special thanks to my wife Ana and my son David who make all my hard work worthwhile.

PREFACE

Thank you for choosing this book. I sincerely believe that if you follow my advice you'll significantly improve your chances of making $ERIOUS MONEY online.

I've spent the last twelve years of my life developing online businesses from concept to completion and I've help set up over seventy e-commerce websites, many of which are the most profitable in their market sector. I honestly believe that I now know as much about what works and what doesn't work regarding making money online as anyone in the business. I now want to share that knowledge with you.

The purpose of this book is to help you:

1. **Choose A Profitable Online Business** - by comparing your proposed online business model against proven business models, outlining which products and services sell online and suggesting proven online opportunities.

2. **Eliminate The Risk Associated With Starting Any Business** - by testing and researching specific market sectors using advanced online testing and market research techniques, as well as emulating real world case studies.

3. **Avoid The Common Pitfalls Of Starting And Maintaining An Online Business** - by comparing your business proposal against successful strategies and summarizing the 'best practice' business techniques used by most successful internet companies.

Good Luck!

Dr. Richard G. Lewis FCIM
www.riskeliminator.com

PARTS OF THIS BOOK

PART ONE: CHOOSE YOUR WEAPONS

This section will help you come up with a business idea and decide whether it is likely to succeed. I'll explain the preparation needed to make your online business a success, including: idea generation, market research, the *Risk Eliminator*™ system, as well as the importance of the *Keyword Continuum*™ and a *Unique Proposition Strategy*™.

PART TWO: DON'T RE-INVENT THE WHEEL!

Here you'll learn to develop a business model that really works. This section outlines the Internet-based businesses that are already profitable, as well as predicting which businesses will be profitable in the future. It explains how to use the *Strategic Fit Matrix*™ to help define and evaluate which businesses have the correct *Strategic Fit*™ for e-commerce, as well as using proven business models and real-life case studies. It also has a comprehensive list of online opportunities you may be interested in.

PART THREE: THE GOLDEN SECRETS OF BUSINESS SUCCESS

This section will help you stay in business long enough to make $ERIOUS MONEY! Here you'll learn the best business practices about running an online business, as well as detailed practical advice that is relevant to any business. You'll learn the importance of having a successful model to follow or a support system or team behind you. You'll also learn the advantages of using *Strategic Synergy*™ and affiliates to promote your venture.

CONTENT

PART ONE
CHOOSE YOUR WEAPONS

Chapter One

Chapter Two

Chapter Three

PART THREE
THE GOLDEN SECRETS OF BUSINESS SUCCESS

Chapter Eight

Chapter Nine

Chapter Ten

Chapter Sixteen

Chapter Seventeen

Chapter Eighteen

INTRODUCTION

It's a fact; the most likely way of making a million is not by buying a lottery ticket or investing in stock or property. Other than inheriting money, the way that most people become rich is by owning a successful business. Running a business is never easy but fortune favors the brave, and the rewards can be huge.

"You will never do anything in this world without courage.
It is the greatest quality of the mind next to honor."
Aristotle

Often, the hardest part about starting a business is coming up with an idea for a business or choosing a product or service that will sell or, more importantly, finding customers that want to buy what you are selling. After all, if you get it wrong, it can be an extremely expensive mistake! That's why it's so important to do your research and choose the correct option.

"The beginning is the most important part of the work."
Plato

Using the advice, examples, case studies, techniques and tools in this book you'll learn how to significantly improve your chances of establishing a profitable online business. By researching your target market and testing your marketing message, you'll be able to set realistic, achievable goals.

"A goal properly set is halfway reached."
Zig Ziglar

There are many reasons why people start their own business. Only you'll know if it is the right time to start a business, but it is a fact that most successful business people are not exceptionally smart – the smartest thing they ever do is take the right advice – that's the purpose of this book; to show you how to make $ERIOUS MONEY online!

You'll Make $ERIOUS
MONEY Online!

PART ONE

CHOOSE YOUR WEAPONS

Chapter One

Why the Internet?

WHY SHOULD YOU START AN ONLINE BUSINESS?

If you're serious about securing your financial future then an online business can be the least risky, most profitable, and most enjoyable option.

Top Reasons Why People Start Their Own Business:

1. Freedom
2. Wealth
3. Fulfillment

Obviously, if you follow the right advice it is much more probable that you'll succeed. However, we all know that it is often other qualities that determine our success or failure.

> "The will to win, the desire to succeed, the urge to reach your full potential... these are the keys that will unlock the door to personal excellence."
> Confucius

Rather than concentrating on the positives, very often success comes from avoiding the negative influences. Before you embark on any business venture, it's a good idea to be aware of the pitfalls you may encounter.

Top Reasons Why People Fail:

1. Business Too Dependent on Owner
2. Exhaustion
3. Not Enough Capital
4. Not Enough Expertise
5. Failure to Ask for Help
6. Distractions

Very often the best way to start a business is part time, from home, while you maintain your day job. Thousands of successful entrepreneurs and online business people have started in this way; step-by-step.

> "It does not matter how slowly you go as long as you do not stop."
>
> Confucius

The important thing is to make the change as soon as possible. Seize the opportunity and start the process today; follow the advice in this book and commercial success could be yours quicker than you think.

> "Opportunities multiply as they are seized."
>
> Sun Tzu

IN THE PLACE TO BE

And the best place to start any business these days? On the Internet! It is without exception the cheapest, most cost-effective channel to market the world of commerce has ever known. No other marketplace can offer comparable means of accurately testing or measuring your advertising, your conversion rates, your customers' usage paths, your marketing messages etc. etc.

The next few years will see a huge take up of the Internet throughout the world. Most experts are predicting a 200%+ global increase in the number of Internet users and broadband provision over the next three to five years as the various world economies fulfill their various economic 'stimulation packages' by providing the infrastructure for fast Internet usage. This will provide the biggest retail audience the world has ever seen.

The Internet also provides a small business with the means to compete with larger corporations. If you can provide a high quality product or service to a niche target market; backed up with good customer service and delivery, added-value and exceptional product knowledge, you'll make $ERIOUS MONEY online!

THE INTERNET

If you're serious about starting a business that can make lots of money quickly, then the Internet is the place to be. Compared to any other channel to market in history the Internet is the cheapest in which to test, set-up, launch, maintain and market your business. It also has a huge potential market and can reduce your costs and provide a higher level of customer care.

There are currently over 6 million small businesses in the United States and based on what you hear in the news and by talking with others, you might assume that everyone who has a business has a website for e-commerce. Amazingly, the truth is that approximately 67.8% of small businesses *don't* sell any products or services online. What an opportunity to step in and dominate your market sector!

Business has never been better; according to most reputable studies, online retail sales will rise 17 percent in 2009 to $192.1 billion.

PLATE 1: US ONLINE RETAIL REVENUES

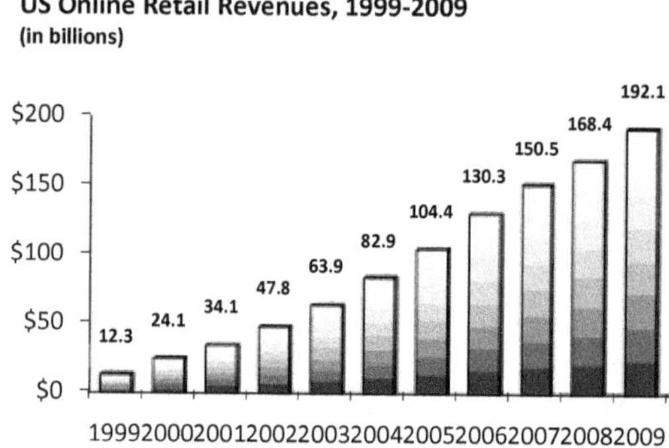

Note: Excludes Travel, Prescription Drugs & Auto (US Only)

HOW TO MAKE $*ERIOUS MONEY* ONLINE

Here are the two most important secrets to making *$ERIOUS MONEY* online:

Secret #1: Choose Your Weapons Carefully

Whereas many offline companies in the same sector sell identical products and services as other businesses but can still compete through better location, price, promotions, customer service, marketing etc., online companies are different. Because all online companies are basically competing in the same 'neighborhood' the most important prerequisite to be successful online is to provide a product or service that is popular enough to be profitable (seems obvious, eh?).

Therefore, nothing has a bigger influence on your success, than the choice of what you decide to sell or the customers you target. The best designed website or marketing strategy or affiliate program won't mean a thing if no one wants to buy what you have got to sell.

Now, thanks to my advice and the techniques I will show you, you can identify profitable products or services that will sell well online.

Secret #2: Find Your Pot of Gold

> "The only way left to make serious money online seems
> to be by selling a product or service that appeals to an
> under-serviced but profitable niche."
>
> Ben Black

That statement may also seem obvious but unlike traditional commerce, if you can't compete with huge multinational brands, then you'd better find a product or service that no one else is selling online or a niche market no one is servicing; a 'pot of gold' no one else has yet found.

The truth is if you choose a high demand product or service that fulfills a high-demand, under-fulfilled niche, you can expect to make serious money, very quickly.

Now that e-commerce is mature enough to have countless different businesses competing in most commercial sectors, the best way to ensure a profitable online business is to identify and dominate a profitable and previously under-serviced market sector.

As with any business, if you discover a niche first, you have a greater chance of capturing the largest market share, and gaining 'first-mover advantage'. Fortunately, most online market sectors can be segmented into a niche market sector, as you'll see from the companies highlighted in the *Strategic Fit Matrix*™ (see PART TWO: DON'T RE-INVENT THE WHEEL!).

To concentrate your business operation on one market niche means to specialize in that specific sector. Consequently, the more you specialize, the more you reduce your prospective customer base. Obviously, this means that rather than appealing to the broad spectrum of all Internet users, your products or services only appeal to a select, specific customer.

However, if that niche has fewer direct competitors, it does have the potential to be profitable. If it is profitable and offers the opportunity for repeat sales, multiple sales, up-sales, cross-sales and complimentary goods sales, then it should be extremely profitable – it's up to you to exploit it!

> "If you can dream it, then you can achieve it."
> Zig Ziglar

CAN YOUR HOBBY MAKE YOU RICH?

Imagine making money from your hobby or doing something you really enjoy doing. Wouldn't that be a wonderful, life-changing event?

> "Choose a job you love, and you will never have to work a day in your life."
> Confucius

Imagine stress-free living, and actually looking forward to starting work every day; not wanting to go to bed because you were enjoying what you were doing so much! I know what that feels like because I do it!

> "Some people find an interest in making money, and though they appear to be slaving, many actually enjoy every minute of their work."
> Walter Annenberg

This is the perfect combination for a successful business idea:

> 1. **Passion** (something you have had a deep passion for or interested in for a long time)
> 2. **Expertise** (a product, service or subject you know in depth)
> 3. **Demand** (enough Internet users are also interested in the subject to provide a sufficiently large potential customer base)

It's important that the business you go into is not just one that you think will make money, but you have no interest in; you have to maintain enthusiasm in your business to maintain growth.

> "The greatest happiness comes from being vitally interested in something that excites all your energies."
> Walter Annenberg

With enthusiasm comes knowledge, with knowledge comes expertise. If you have a passion and expertise in a subject then you'll put in more hours, and customers will enjoy your enthusiasm and pay for your knowledge and expertise. These are potent ingredients for any successful, enjoyable business.

> "Making money is a hobby that will complement any other hobbies you have, beautifully."
> Scott Alexander.

PASSION PAYS

The Passion Principle: **N + P + D = \$erious Money***

* N = niche, P = passion, D = demand for product or service.

Without a passion for what you do, you'll soon falter and so will your business. After all, potentially, you may have to spend 12 to 18 hours every day working on your business, often for the first one or two years.

> "Without passion you don't have energy, without energy you have nothing."
>
> Donald Trump

You have to constantly be thinking about ways to improve and grow your business, as well as talking about it to everyone, everywhere. If you start a venture that you are not passionate about it will be difficult to put in the hours and energy to make it successful.

> "The more I want to get something done, the less I call it work."
>
> Richard Bach

What are you passionate about? Try listing all the things you are interested in, then make a list of the things on that list that you are passionate about. Then prioritize; what are you *most* passionate about? Know who you are; know your strengths and weaknesses, know that you are ready, willing and able to invest the time, energy and money necessary to make your venture a success.

> "Pleasure in the job puts perfection in the work."
>
> Aristotle

Let's say your passion is photography. People pay for solutions to a problem, therefore you need to find out what problems photographers have and how to solve or alleviate that problem.

The best place to do this is to research the photography forums and evaluate the needs of your potential customers. Obviously, if you are interested in this area you'll no doubt share many of the frustrations, needs and wants with other enthusiasts.

> "Without passion man is a mere latent force and possibility, like the flint which awaits the shock of the iron before it can give forth its spark."
> Henri Frederic Amiel

For example, imagine you chose underwater or waterproof digital cameras, as used by sports enthusiasts, holiday makers and scuba divers etc. as the product you are really enthusiastic and knowledgeable about - this might make a good choice of online business. The more you specialize in this specific niche the more likely you are to be successful.

You'll Make $ERIOUS
MONEY Online!

Chapter Two

Getting Started

IDEA GENERATION (IDEATION)

If you haven't got a hobby or are not passionate about something, then maybe you've got an outstanding idea for a business.

> "As long as you're going to be thinking anyway, think big."
> Donald Trump

Most people who come up with a great idea for a business do so by thinking about their own lives and what product or service they wish was available to them that would make their lives better. Another common way of identifying a gap in the market is when a product or service you want is not available online.

> "Necessity... the mother of invention."
> Plato

Think simple. Great ideas are often the simplest ones. By thinking of your simplest recurring need, and how you can fulfill it, you can come up with a business idea that also fulfills the needs of others.

If you have a business idea, don't try to develop it around what you think potential customers will like or need. Instead, find out what people *actually* want or need. Too often business owners get an idea in their head and jump right in with both feet. However, they soon find out that their target market does not want what they are offering.

> "You will get all you want in life if you help enough
> other people get what they want."
> Zig Ziglar

Getting out and understand potential customers may lead you to the perfect idea. Knowing what potential consumers need and building products to meet those needs is a good business idea.

Try brainstorming with other people; talk to family, friends, etc. See if anyone else has any great ideas. They may not be starting a business or even own one, but they may have a great idea for one. Getting input from other people can definitely help as they may well end up being your customers.

> "A person with a new idea is a crank until the
> idea succeeds."
>
> Mark Twain

Research online. Try to research online what others who have a business have done. You may find a great idea or technique that has not been used in your chosen sector. Or, if you have no idea what kind of business to start, try looking online and finding success stories. There may be a great idea or a franchise you can start.

You can then test the idea out to see if there is enough demand for that product or service to make it a profitable proposition. If you do have a great business idea that becomes successful it could make you very rich indeed, especially if you fully exploit your first-mover advantage.

> "If you want to be successful, it's just this simple. Know
> what you are doing. Love what you are doing. And
> believe in what you are doing."
>
> Will Rogers

NEVER BE THE FIRST THROUGH THE DOOR

The first person through the door gets shot; the guys that follow learn from that mistake.

> "In the modern world of business, it is useless to be a creative, original thinker unless you can also sell what you create."
>
> David Ogilvy

Don't be a vanguard, unless it's a simple, easily-fulfilled service or you've got enough money and infrastructure behind you to educate your prospective customers and fulfill their demands, as well as provide spare parts and/or the after-sales service required to support your product or service.

New products or services are rarely successful due to the fact that your potential customers have to be educated as to the benefit to them. Initially, there will not immediately be a network of support systems or services, replacement parts, repair shops etc. to back up your invention. Also, producing products in enough numbers to be profitable is costly and marketing them can be extremely expensive, until sufficient customers use it.

> "Any new technology tends to go through a 25-year adoption cycle."
>
> Marc Andreessen

Neither Microsoft, Google nor eBay invented anything, nor did they create the sector they dominate. They just made their product or service 1% better than their competition. Rather than come up with a completely new idea, research what people are looking to purchase now and give it to them cheaper, quicker, with better customer service and with more added value.

TO TEST IS BEST

"Success depends upon previous preparation, and without such preparation there is sure to be failure."
Confucius

Researching your subject, testing different offers and measuring responses are the proven tools to uncovering the truth about what your potential customers really want.

"As a small businessperson, you have no greater leverage than the truth."
John Greenleaf Whittier

Do you think you have come up with a unique idea for a product or service that will sell well online? A risk or feasibility study is a well-proven course to take to accurately predict if that idea will be successful.

Feasibility Study Process:

1. Idea > Research > Test > Survey > Research > Feedback > Write Copy > Test > Design Website > Test > Feedback > Review > Changes > Test.
2. If successful, write a business plan and add a selling infrastructure (bank account, credit card processing, more stock, delivery and fulfillment etc.)
3. Develop a selling strategy: up-selling, cross-selling, repeat selling, bundling products etc.
4. Create a 'competitor' (see PART THREE: THE GOLDEN SECRETS OF BUSINESS SUCCESS).

"Business, more than any other occupation, is a continual dealing with the future; it is a continual calculation, an instinctive exercise in foresight."
Henry R. Luce

WHAT SHOULD YOU SELL?

How can you tell if your business idea is right for e-commerce? It depends upon what you sell. If you already have a business or are contemplating starting an online business, you need to look at your products and/or services to decide if they fit the Internet model of buying. Not everything sells well online.

People buy products online that they don't need to smell, touch or examine. They want products that they are fairly familiar with or products that don't carry an element of surprise upon receiving them. In other words, they have a pretty good idea of what it is they are getting.

For example, online bookstores like Amazon.com do well because those buying a book don't need to hold the book to know something about it. Plus, online bookstores offer feedback that bookstores don't, such as reviews, ratings, and extensive descriptions. Add to this fast and easy shipping and you have found a market and retail model that works well online. This same concept also holds true for generic goods such as music, DVDs, electronic goods etc.

Another example is travel. Using the Internet is easier than making a trip to a travel agency. If you are going on a cruise, you can view photos and floor plans, see photos from various excursions, get price quotes and sailing dates. You can even compare prices among several different agencies and then book your cruise online. You know exactly what you should be getting.

Items that are hard to find also sell well online. If you offer a unique product that can't be found in stores, people are more likely to purchase through a company website. It makes sense that common products that you can buy at the local store don't sell well online, but if you can identify unique products and advertise those products to their target markets you may have a winner.

Also, unique, rare, authentic or specialized products and services are always popular online.

YOU WON'T GO FAR WITHOUT IPR

If you have generated a unique money-making idea or invention then you should protect it from being copied or abused by competitors.

PLATE 2: IP PROTECTION WEBSITE

There are three major types of Intellectual Property (IP):

- Copyright
- Patents
- Trademarks

COPYRIGHT

If you produce anything that is unique and creative, be it software, an image, a book or music, you can immediately and automatically have copyright over it; you don't need to register it. Also, you can legally protect your creativity against anyone who uses it without your permission.

PATENTS

Patents are used to protect inventions such as a physical machine that solves a problem or provides a unique solution. To be granted a patent you'll have to prove that the invention is useful and unique and provide detailed drawings of its design.

TRADEMARKS

A Trademark is a mark under which you trade your goods and services e.g. a logo. You can add a TM symbol after your trademark to reserve it, or you can use the ® symbol once you have legally registered your trademark.

Whatever your idea is, to make money from it online you had better protect it and make use of it as quickly as possible as things on the Internet move very quickly.

"Intellectual property has the shelf life of a banana."
Bill Gates

You'll Make $ERIOUS
MONEY Online!

Chapter Three

What to Sell Online

SO WHAT EXACTLY *DO* PEOPLE WANT?

One of the best ways to determine what to sell is to find products that meet the basic needs of people. The good news is that what people need and want will remain the same for the rest of your lifetime. The technology for delivering those needs may change but human desires won't.

Therefore, all you need to do is figure out what people want and you can profit from their desires. And, since their desires are predictable, your ability to make money from your ideas just got a lot more bankable as well.

So, what exactly do people want? Abraham Maslow came up with a theory over 50 years ago that still stands today, known as *Maslow's Hierarchy of Needs*. It has become one of the most popular and often-cited theories of human motivation.

PLATE 3: MASLOW'S HIERARCHY OF NEEDS

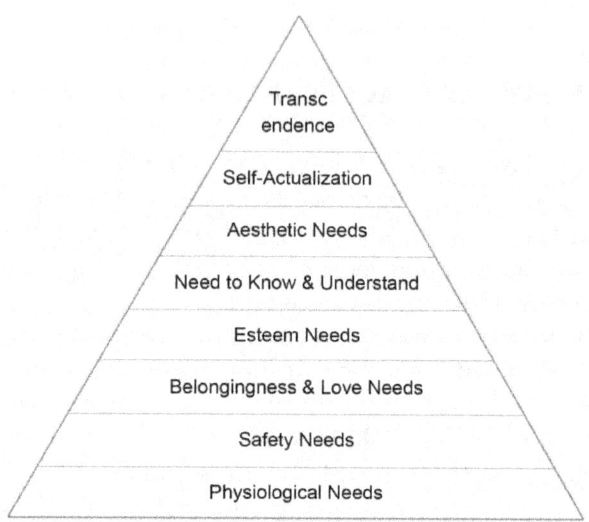

Maslow explains that humans must fulfill need number one before they will consider need number two, and so on. A person won't try to fulfill needs higher up the chain because the early desires are required for survival. He suggests the following eight needs:

1) **Physiological**: hunger, thirst, bodily comforts, etc

2) **Safety/security**: to keep out of danger

3) **Belongingness and Love**: to affiliate with others or be accepted

4) **Esteem**: to achieve, be competent, gain approval and recognition

5) **Cognitive**: to know, to understand, and explore

6) **Aesthetic**: appreciating symmetry, order, and beauty

7) **Self-actualization**: to find self-fulfillment and realize one's potential

8)   **Self-transcendence**: to connect to something beyond the ego or to help others find self-fulfillment and realize their potential.

Our three highest-level needs (6, 7 and 8) are satisfied by: money, sex and food (not necessarily in that order).

Therefore, there will always be a market for websites with any subject that helps the customer become more attractive to the opposite sex (e.g. dieting, clothes or make up) or that helps people to make money. Also, websites such as dating agencies and cooking are always popular. These needs will never change, ever. So if you have an idea that fits in one of those categories, and if it's a new spin on existing ideas, you are very likely to be successful.

If you fulfill a customer's self-actualization (number seven on the Hierarchy of Needs) and allow them to find self-fulfillment and realize their potential, then you have tapped into the pervading psychology of the new consumer that dominates online.

> "Human behavior flows from three main sources: desire, emotion, and knowledge."
>
> Plato

DO YOU FULFILL YOUR CUSTOMERS' NEEDS?

Here are some purchasing motives that fit into Maslow's hierarchy. These motives are shown in descending order of need. They include:

1. To make money
2. To save money
3. To save time
4. To avoid effort or make work easier
5. To be more comfortable
6. To achieve greater cleanliness/hygiene
7. To be healthier
8. To be pain free
9. To gain praise
10. To be popular
11. To attract sex
12. To keep/safeguard your possessions
13. To have more fun
14. To satisfy curiosity
15. To protect your family
16. To be in style
17. To acquire new/beautiful possessions
18. To quench your appetite
19. To emulate others
20. To avoid trouble
21. To avoid criticism
22. To be an individual
23. To protect your reputation
24. To grab opportunities
25. To be safe

Since these motives are related to the needs and desires of people everywhere, choosing a product related to any of the 25 needs above will give you a better chance of having a successful online business.

DOES YOUR BUSINESS IDEA FIT THE INTERNET?

Now that you know what sells online, it is time to determine if your company and its way of doing business actually fit the characteristics needed for selling online. This is known as *Strategic Fit™*. As a small business owner/manager, determining whether or not your business has the correct *Strategic Fit™* for e-commerce will be one of the most critical judgments you must make.

The fact is, if you know in advance that your business concept doesn't have the products, services or processes necessary to be successful online, wouldn't it be sensible to either fix those deficiencies or concentrate on a different product, service, or channel to market?

As a small business, you are not likely to be a "Wal-Mart of the Internet." Instead, you'll probably operate with a small number of products or services, aimed at a relatively small market; in comparison to the 875 million Internet shoppers currently available. You are also likely to have a greater need for a competitive edge since you'll be competing with others with similar businesses.

> "The key to competing and surviving against Wal-Mart is to focus your business into a niche or pocket where you can leverage your strengths."
>
> Michael Bergdahl

If the product or service your company has to offer does not appeal to the current Internet audience then setting up an Internet presence will only serve as a frustrating drain of your business' cash. That is why it is necessary to understand who uses the Internet and who is buying what.

According to recent research (2009), the percentage of men and women users is essentially the same, as are the differences among races. The biggest differences lie in income and education. Therefore, to have the highest number of potential shoppers, your products or services should be aimed at educated individuals with an income of $75K or higher. Unless you have identified a specific profitable niche outside this demographic, if you don't provide a product or service that appeals to the specific group of consumers found online then it has little chance of being successful.

Internet Usage Among North Americans

Percentage of Use in Each Group:

Total Adults

Women	70%
Men	71%

Age

18-29	87%
30-49	83%
50-64	65%
65+	32%

Race/Ethnicity

White, Non-Hispanic	73%
Black, Non-Hispanic	62%
English-speaking Hispanic	78%

Geography

Urban	73%
Suburban	73%
Rural	60%

Income (Household)

Less than $30,000/yr	55%
$30,000-49,999	69%
$50,000-$74,999	88%
$75,000+	93%

Educational Attainment

Less than High School	40%
High School	61%
Attended Some College	81%
College+	91%

Consideration should be made as to whether your business idea is commercially sound (i.e. if it will make you money) and whether it will "fit" the audience most likely to purchase on the Internet.

WHAT SELLS ONLINE

So which businesses actually have the correct "fit" for Internet commerce? The obvious candidates for successful e-commerce are simple, recognizable products or services that are easily understood. Once you determine the product or service you want to sell, then you have to consider whether your target market fits the profile of the typical web audience.

Top 10 Products Purchased Online:

1. Tickets (Travel/Concert/Theatre/Festival/Cinema)
2. Holidays
3. Books
4. Computer Hardware
5. Clothes
6. Electrical Goods
7. CDs/DVDs/Music Downloads
8. Computer Software
9. Drugs/Health and Beauty Aids
10. Toys/Hobby goods and Games

WHAT DOESN'T SELL ONLINE

The following list highlights those Internet promotions that do *not* have the *Strategic Fit*™ for e-commerce:

1. Generic products or services freely available, easily obtainable, and for the same price elsewhere

2. Products or services that do not appeal to the Internet audience

3. New products that are not understood by prospective buyers

4. Products that need pre-sales service to explain the benefits

5. Products that disregard the customers' needs

6. Products limited by their geographical range

7. Product promotion that annoys customers with uninteresting information

8. Websites that download slowly because of excessive use of technology

9. Businesses that misjudge the value customers give to a product

10. Businesses that fail to enhance the product or service with added value and information

HOW YOU CAN MAKE MONEY ONLINE

Most research suggests that there are basically three ways to make money online:

1. Selling of goods or services.

2. Selling advertising.

3. Reselling goods or services.

If you decide to go online and you have formulated an Internet-related business plan, consideration should be made as to what risks you are willing to take and how you are going to measure your company's success against its objectives.

The costs involved in trading over the Internet range significantly, therefore you have to evaluate how much you can afford to spend. However, if your products or services fit the Internet consumer profile then you may be well on your way to making $ERIOUS MONEY!

You'll Make $ERIOUS
MONEY Online!

Chapter Four

How to Find a Pot of Gold

HOW DO I IDENTIFY AN ONLINE NICHE?

How can you find out if your business idea will make money online? At last, using the *Risk Eliminator*™ system, and its in-depth use of online market research, you can predict with outstanding accuracy the demand for your product or service before you even spend a single penny on development.

> "Risk comes from not knowing what you're doing."
> Warren Buffett

Now that you've identified which products and services sell online, and which businesses have the *Strategic Fit*™ for e-commerce, it's now time to test if your own specific business idea is likely to successful.

THE *RISK ELIMINATOR*™ SYSTEM

To test the potential of your business idea you'll have to conduct some online market research. Without exception, market research is the most important factor in predicting whether or not your online business will be a success. It will save you $1,000s and increase any potential profit by $1,000s, probably $1,000,000s.

Thankfully, online market research has become a simple, inexpensive, and incredibly precise predictive business tool. The advent of pay-per-click advertising media, such as Yahoo! Search Marketing and Google AdWords, has made the measurement and testing of the online demand for products and service extremely accurate.

Plate 4: Yahoo! Small Business Website

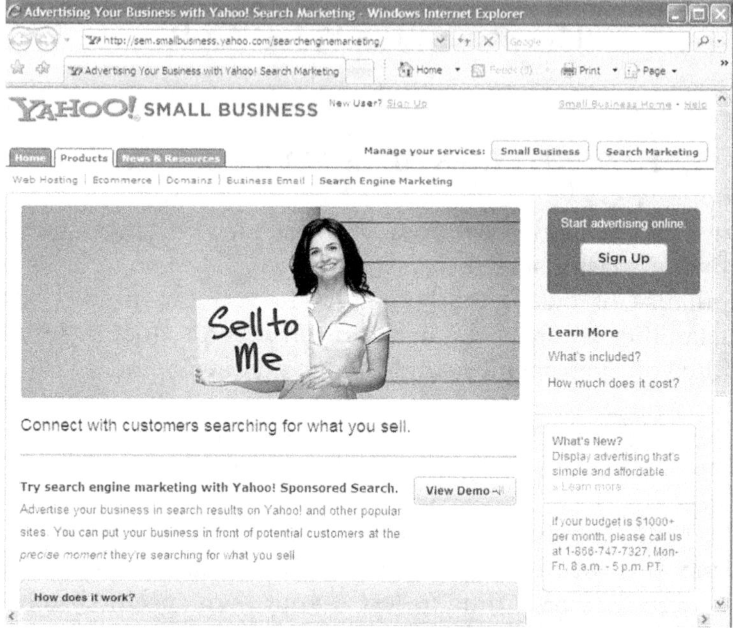

Initial Research and Development

Before you initiate your online market research, analyze your business idea and quantify the benefits it will offer your target market. Do conventional research in your proposed area of specialty by reading industry periodicals, blogs from industry leaders, and investigating any competitors.

Competitor analysis is essential. Every business has competition, either direct or indirect. Some competitors are ruthless, so be very careful about analyzing the competitors in your chosen industry sector before entering it.

> "The competitor to be feared is one who never bothers about you at all, but goes on making his own business better all the time."
>
> Henry Ford

When you feel you have found a niche to test and you know the subject matter well enough (and what the target market that is interested in that subject want to buy), write a short article or white paper that offers some key piece of information about the benefits of your new business idea, product or service without compromising any of your intellectual property. This information will be used as the 'bait' to acquire a response from your target prospects.

"The finer the bait, the shorter the wait!"
Frank Gorshin

ONLINE MARKET RESEARCH

To eliminate as much risk as possible, long before you launch your website, or even start designing it, you should conduct the following research:

1. **Test Keywords**
2. **Test PPC**
3. **Use Web-based Surveys**
4. **Analyze Survey Data**
5. **Design (Keyword-Specific) Landing Pages**

The first piece of data you need to establish is if there is a sufficient monthly volume of potential customers actively searching for the product or service you propose selling online. It will also be to your advantage if you can determine if other businesses are already making money from those products or services.

To do this you can use keyword research tools like Google AdWords Keyword Tool (https://adwords.google.com/select/KeywordToolExternal) and Yahoo's Keyword Selector Tool (http://searchmarketing.yahoo.com/rc/srch/) along with search engines like Google and Ask. The latter has a useful 'Related Searches' prompt in the right hand sidebar that will speed up your task considerably.

PLATE 5: GOOGLE ADWORDS WEBSITE

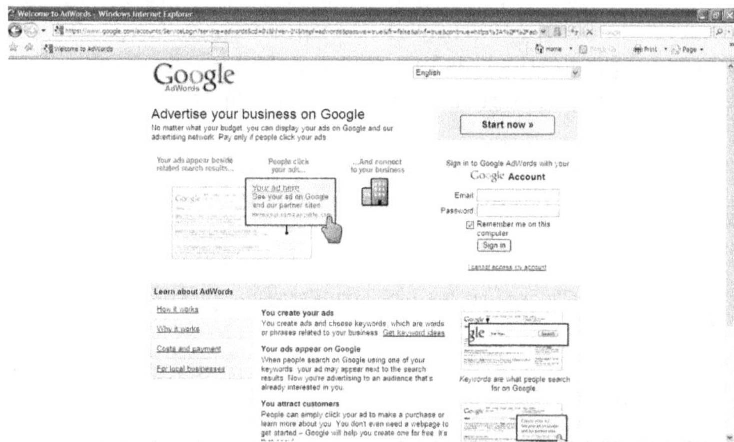

You can also use online resources such as Overture (inventory.overture.com) or WordTracker (wordtracker.com) to conduct market research based on the past behavior of search engine users.

PLATE 6: WORDTRACKER WEBSITE

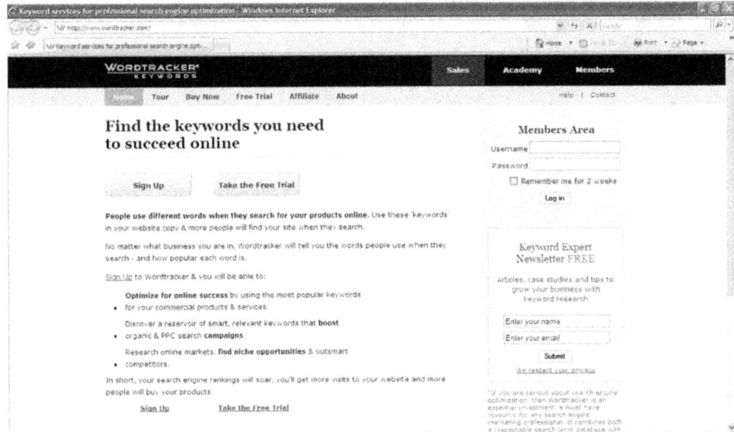

1. TEST KEYWORDS

a. Decide on your keywords from the research conducted using the Overture or WordTracker resources.

PLATE 7: WORDTRACKER SUGGESTION TOOL

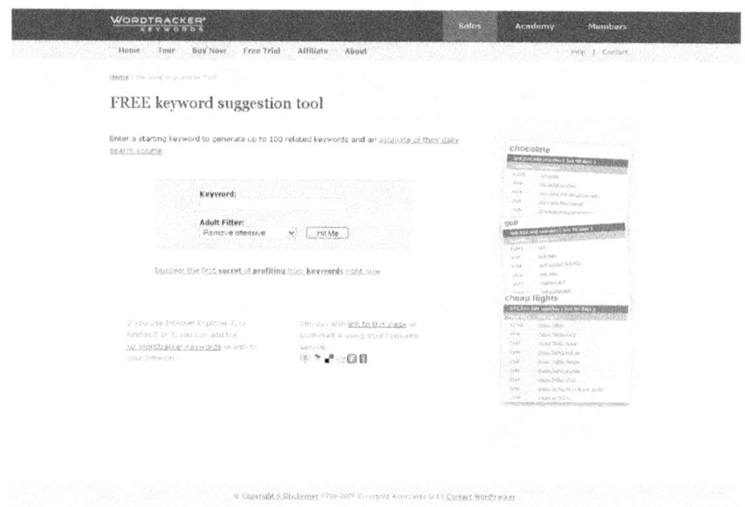

Using either of these resources you can estimate (i) the amount of potential visitor traffic, (ii) which keywords people are using, and (iii) associated keywords that give you clues as to your customer's other requirements.

> "Research is formalized curiosity. It is poking and prying with a purpose."
>
> Zora Neale Hurston

Your research should be focused and deep, testing as many keywords as is practical until you think you have covered every keyword or key phrase that a potential customer would use to search for your product or service.

PLATE 8: WORDTRACKER KEYWORD RESULTS

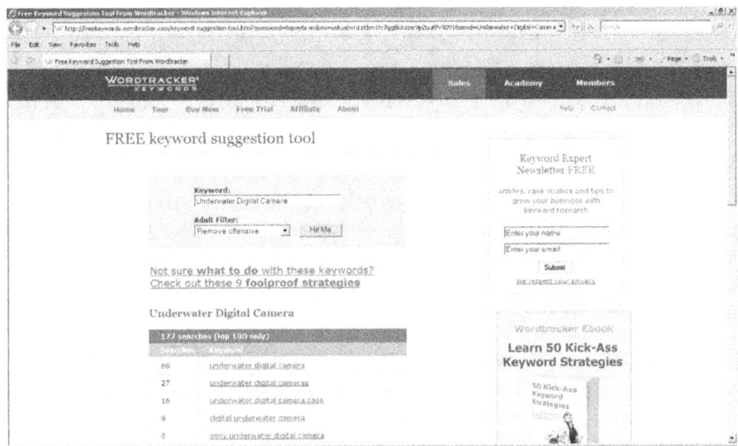

b. Organize your keywords into groups by breaking all your keywords down into groups of specific keywords and phrases; for example, 'underwater digital cameras' in one group and 'underwater digital camera case' in another.

> Group 1:
> 69 underwater digital camera
> 27 underwater digital cameras
> 9 digital underwater camera
>
> Group 2:
> 16 underwater digital camera case

Try to divide separate keywords into groups of no less than 2,000 searches per month (preferably 4,000+). For example, 69 + 27 + 9 = 105 (105 searches related to 'underwater camera'). 105 x 28 = 2,940 searches for 'underwater camera' per month.

The purpose of doing this is to find a common mindset of groups of people that are looking for similar products, services, information, benefits or features. These groups will later be separated into different Ad Groups in Google.

The most popular keywords will later be used in your advertisement messages and form part of the *Keyword*

Continuum™ used throughout your marketing campaigns.

2. TEST PPC

Set up accounts and campaigns with either Yahoo! Search Marketing or Google AdWords, keeping your "cost-per-click" as low as possible. If your keyword research was effective, you should be able to get traffic for a free product like your article for between $0.15 and $0.25 per click.

PLATE 9: GOOGLE KEYWORD TOOL WEBSITE

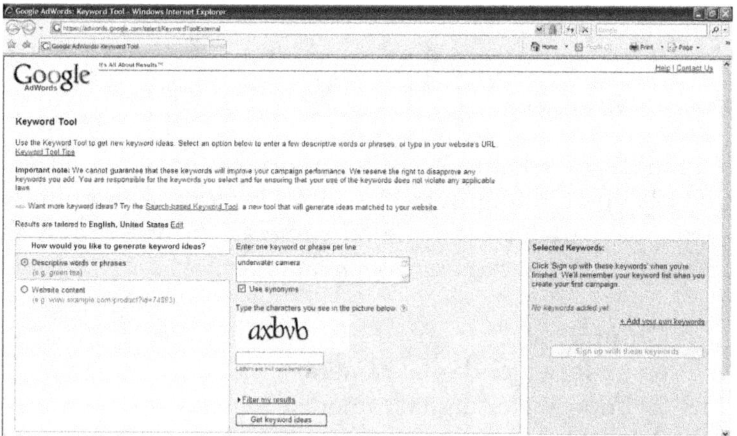

By testing response to sponsorship advertisements in Google, known as "PPC" (Pay Per Click) advertisements, you can estimate whether or not there is sufficient demand for your product or service and if competitors are already making money in this marketplace. You can also estimate potential profit and, if you decide to enter that market, decide how you should "position" your product or service within the market.

> "The most important word in the vocabulary of
> advertising is TEST. If you pre-test your product
> with consumers, and pre-test your advertising, you
> will do well in the marketplace."
>
> David Ogilvy

This research will also help you prioritize your target market, and each segment within it, as well as help estimate your advertising budget. The responses will also help you customize your advertising messages to each separate specific target segment, using the keywords and key phrases they have used to search for your product or service, thus making it more likely to produce an interest in your product or service (i.e. people will 'click' on your advertisement).

> "Never stop testing, and your advertising will never
> stop improving."
>
> David Ogilvy

Using PPC to measure response, demand and costs also helps you to determine several Key Performance Indicators (KPIs), including:

1. **Are any competitors also bidding?** (If not, ask yourself if this is because it is not profitable or because it is a new market, product or service?)
2. **How many competitors?** (Usually, the more competitors, the more profitable the market is)
3. **What is the average bid?**
4. **The difference between bids?**
5. **How long have the competitors been bidding?**

a. You should create a Google Adgroup in Adwords for each keyword group.

Before you start, learn the editorial rules for Yahoo! Search Marketing (http://searchmarketing.yahoo.com/rc/srch/htgla_con.php) or Google AdWords (https://adwords.google.com/select/guidelines.html) and write your first ads using the keywords you discovered during step 1 (Test Keywords).

PLATE 10: GOOGLE SPONSORED ADVERTISEMENT CAMPAIGN

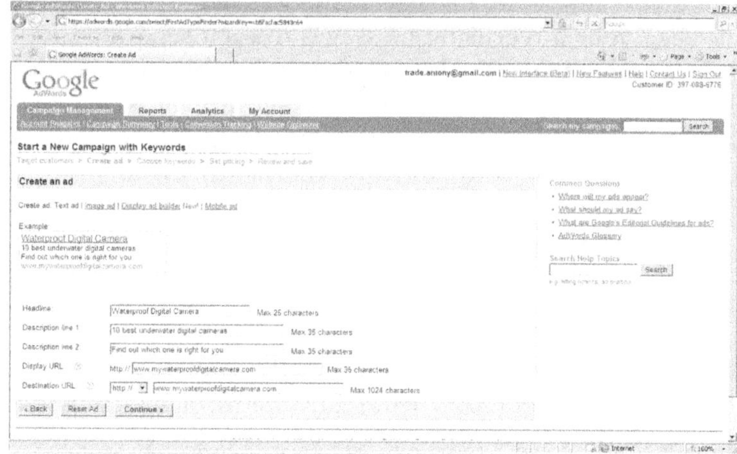

These ads should accurately reflect the content of your article or white paper, or whatever product you advertise, will provide.

PLATE 11: GOOGLE SPONSORED ADVERTISEMENT

b. Run each Ad Group through a test phase and optimize your advertisement copy according to the response to each keyword or key phrase. You can set a differently worded ad for different keywords.

PLATE 12: GOOGLE SPONSORED ADVERTISEMENT KEYWORD SELECTOR

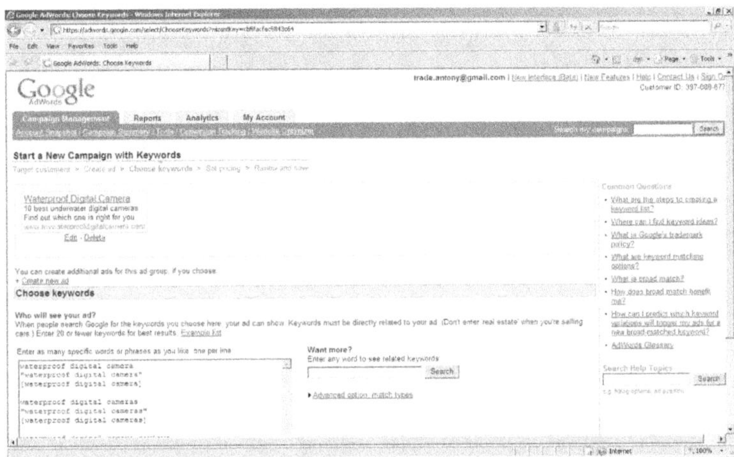

To guarantee a large enough potential market and customer base, most businesses that use these predictive techniques prefer a market that will generate at least 250K searches per month.

PLATE 13: GOOGLE SPONSORED ADVERTISEMENT KEYWORD ANALYZER

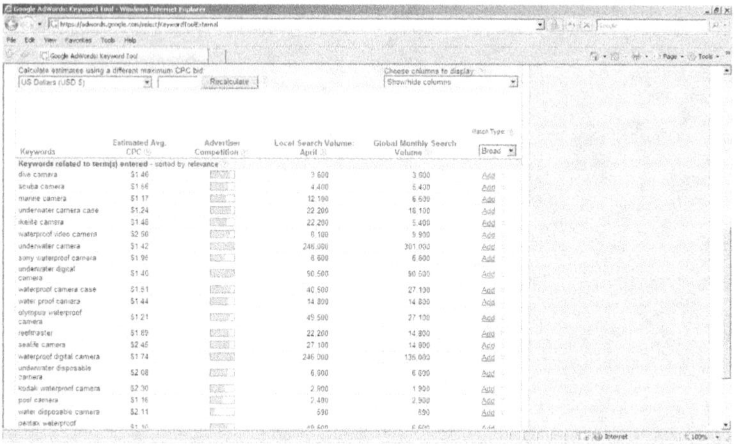

Calculate estimates using a different maximum CPC bid: US Dollars (USD $) Recalculate. Choose columns to display: Show/hide columns.

Keywords	Estimated Avg. CPC	Advertiser Competition	Local Search Volume: April	Global Monthly Search Volume	Match Type: Broad
Keywords related to term(s) entered - sorted by relevance					
dive camera	$1.46		3,600	3,600	Add
scuba camera	$1.66		4,400	6,400	Add
marine camera	$1.17		12,100	6,600	Add
underwater camera case	$1.24		22,200	18,100	Add
ikelite camera	$1.48		22,200	5,400	Add
waterproof video camera	$2.50		8,100	9,900	Add
underwater camera	$1.42		246,000	301,000	Add
sony waterproof camera	$1.96		6,600	6,600	Add
underwater digital camera	$1.40		90,500	90,500	Add
waterproof camera case	$1.51		40,500	27,100	Add
water proof camera	$1.44		14,800	14,800	Add
olympus waterproof camera	$1.21		49,500	27,100	Add
reefmaster	$1.89		22,200	14,800	Add
sealife camera	$2.45		27,100	14,800	Add
waterproof digital camera	$1.74		246,000	135,000	Add
underwater disposable camera	$2.08		6,600	6,600	Add
kodak waterproof camera	$2.30		2,900	1,900	Add
pool camera	$1.16		2,400	2,900	Add
water disposable camera	$2.11		590	590	Add
pentax waterproof	$1.10		49,500	5,600	Add

c. Stop ads which prove too expensive; if the estimated "cost per lead" is too high, given what the average vendor is selling in your market, stop advertising that specific advertisement to that specific market segment.

Note: High bid prices and high volume result in more expensive survey data (and more risk) but may result in higher profit and growth once you have established the business. Most businesses new to this kind of market research start with lower risk, lower volume, and lower price market segments.

3. USE WEB-BASED SURVEYS

If a prospect types in "Waterproof Cameras" into Google and you deliver them a landing page survey instead of a camera they may be annoyed. However, a certain percentage will fill out the survey. People's propensity to fill out a survey is about the same as filling out a form for an e-mail newsletter, which can be a workable number of prospects.

You'll find a different response based on different keywords. Each separate keyword or key phrase you use to attract people to your web page will attract a different "type" of person (i.e. different lifestyle segmentation)

a. Either learn enough HTML to create a basic HTML landing page, or hire a web designer, to produce a web page survey or questionnaire. Use these surveys to ask prospects exactly what they're looking for and how they'd like it prepared, packaged and delivered. Also ask them how much they'd be prepared to spend; this is vitally important as your whole sales strategy will be based on the respondents' opinions.

> "Opinion is the medium between knowledge
> and ignorance."
>
> Plato

The estimated number of sales you can expect can be based upon the number of people that complete the survey (or sign up to your newsletter, white paper etc). Out of the people you sign up you can expect to see between 5% and 10% of the opt-ins to become customers.

You'll then be able to estimate a "cost per sale" based on every keyword in your keyword spread sheet of the market before you commit any more time, money or resources to that specific business.

The cost per lead for each Ad Group is the amount of people prepared to take a survey in proportion to the number of people willing to buy your product or service. The stronger the demand and desire for your product or service, the more probable people are to take the survey.

PLATE 14: ONLINE SURVEY

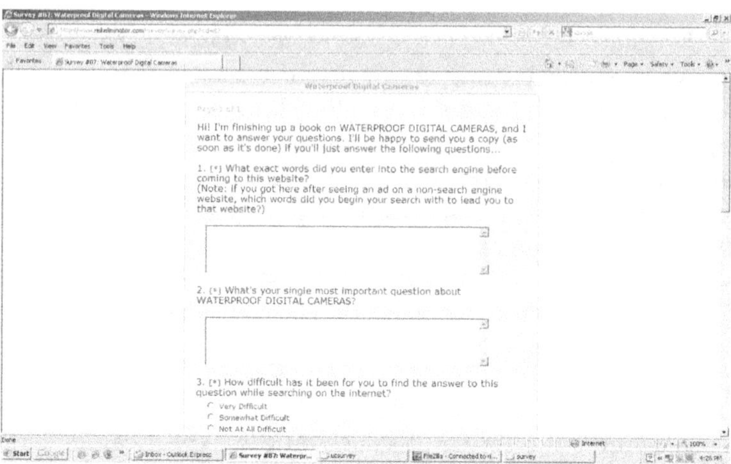

You'll be able to estimate the cost per sale for each sector of the market and the related keyword, as well as estimate which projects are already selling to those keywords, before you make any investments. Using this technique you'll have a very good likelihood of success and know the margins you can obtain should you invest in the business.

b. Now, reset your survey data and collect the full survey. Using this PPC and survey-related research method you can estimate the risk associated with your target market and you can also evaluate what is the motive for using the keywords (i.e. what people really want).

There is a difference between market intelligence and keyword intelligence; market intelligence can be much more valuable; allowing accurate and confident decision-making regarding marketing and strategic decisions.

Aim for 30+ responses in each Ad Group. Use incentives such as the discounts, free downloadable digital products or online services the users expected to find when they clicked on your advertisement.

You should now calculate if there are enough people taking the survey to suggest an affordable response rate:

For Ad Groups which don't produce enough surveys quickly enough, either:
    i) Eliminate from the survey, or
    ii) Decide if they are close enough to other Ad Groups, in mindset, that you can analyze them together later, and let the survey run.

For Ad Groups which do produce enough surveys quickly enough:
    i). Let the survey run, and
    ii). Don't change your PPC advertisements, keyword groups, or traffic pattern. You can do this in the back end analysis (see '4. Analyze Survey Data').

Note: Changing your PPC advertisements after beginning the formal survey data collection can invalidate the entire process by attracting a different segment of people.

DEVICES OTHER THAN SURVEYS

Alternatively, you can use a simple web page using your selling points and keywords from your pay-per-click ads, or hire a designer to set up a simple landing page for you.

The landing page should require a minimum of customer information, such as name and email address. Remember, you can start a dialog and learn more from your website visitors once they decide to trust you with their email address. Include a brief privacy policy that states your intention to protect the security of your visitors' information.

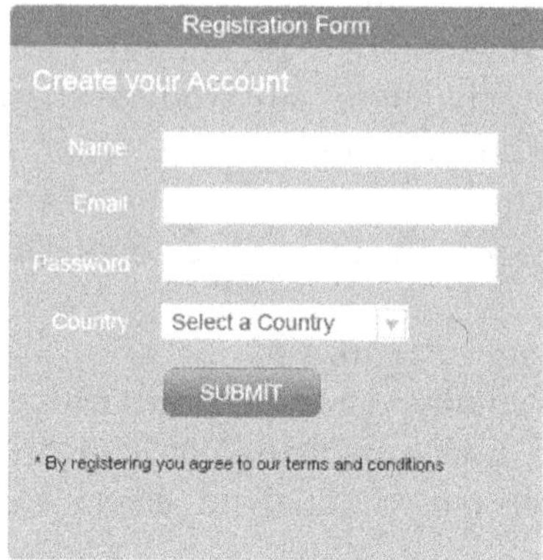

When submitted, the form should send you an email notifying you of the name and email address of the visitor who wants to read your article, newsletter or white paper. If the website proves popular, you'll want to automate this step, but this simple form will be enough to get you started.

4. ANALYZE SURVEY DATA

Now, the challenge is to try to understand exactly why your prospects are searching for specific keywords. This way you can segment the entire market into different segments, which you can target more specifically with your advertising. This alone is a huge competitive advantage should you decide to sell to this market.

a. From the information provided in the web-based surveys, your aim is to provide prospects with (i) exactly what they are looking for, (ii) precisely the way they'd like it, and (iii) at the price they'd be prepared to buy it for. You'll also be able to use the same language they use themselves to write your sales copy.

b. Pre-format your data for analysis and set out your data in a spreadsheet (e.g. MS Excel) in a standard format of one column per question x one row per survey respondent.

PLATE 16: DATA IN SPREAD SHEET (MOST SEARCHED FOR KEYWORDS)

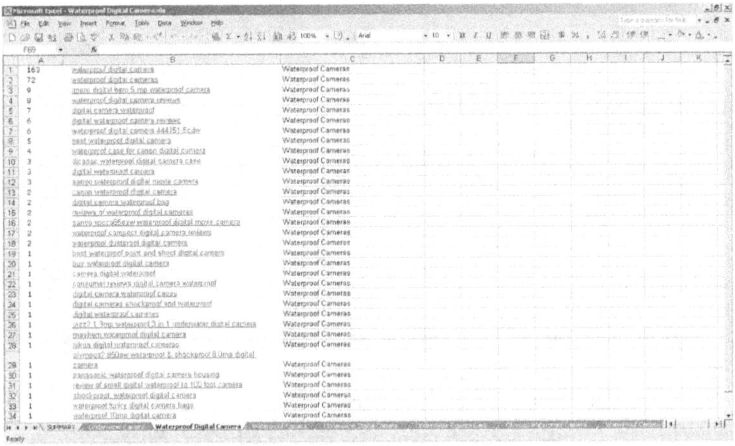

c. You can add a code for each of the open-ended questions and make a code for each unique answer. Then group your codes into higher level categories.

Add a column for each code and each higher level category. You can also add a code for 'Quality' (denoting a high quality respondent) and 'Phone' (denoting a respondent who has given their phone number and is willing to talk to you) to each respondent.

PLATE 17: DATA IN SPREAD SHEET (NUMBER OF SEARCHES)

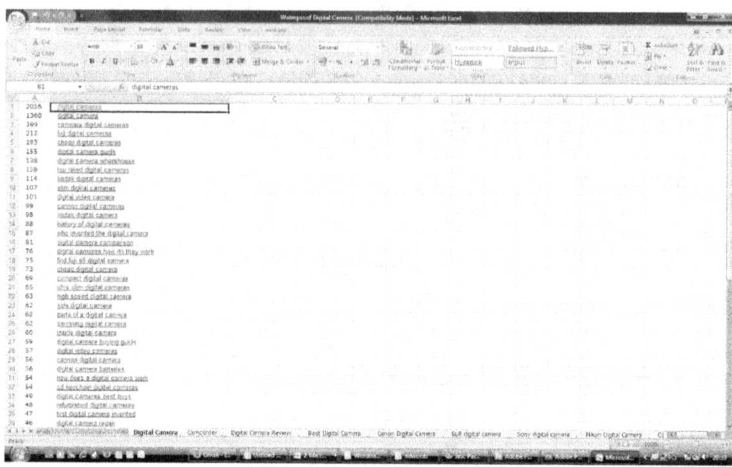

d. Analyze the higher level categories to:
(i) Study the overall frequency (volume) of each category
(ii) Consider which questions are perceived as more difficult to answer
(iii) Examine which concerns are associated with higher quality answers
(iv) Observe which answers are associated with an interest in initiating a relationship or contact, such as the willingness to leave a phone number etc.
(vi) Look for any demographic biases associated with the concerns of the respondent

When you have analyzed all of this data, place it all into a color-coordinated spreadsheet so that you can understand the data at a glance.

PLATE 18: SEGMENTED DATA IN SPREAD SHEET (COLOR COORDINATED)

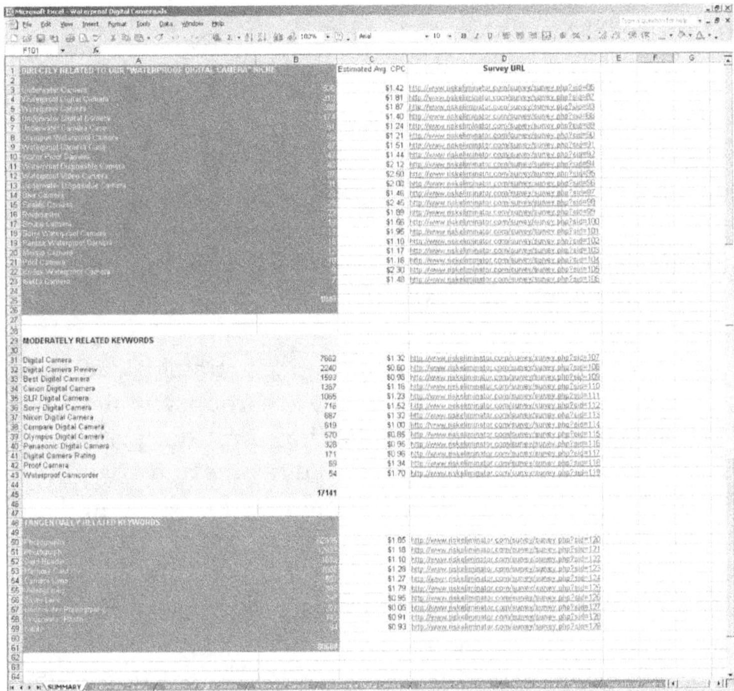

e. Divide your findings segments by working out any correlations between every higher level category of concern and every other higher level category of concern. Then work out any correlations between every higher level category of concern and the major codes for questions such as, "How difficult has it been for you to find the answer to this question while searching on the internet?"

PLATE 19: SURVEY QUESTIONS

3. [*] How difficult has it been for you to find the answer to this question while searching on the internet?

    ◯ Very Difficult

    ◯ Somewhat Difficult

    ◯ Not At All Difficult

Consider which categories are related to one another and look for any relationships that may signify a new segment or may give a clue as to the search terms and phrases the respondents use.

f. Your lead acquisition strategy should be based on your ability to specifically target concerns using PPC and surveys. The data you acquire should help you determine (i) which keywords you bid for, (ii) which Ad Groups you use, (iii) which area of your prospects' concerns you'll prioritize, (iv) which areas you'll treat as secondary concerns, and (v) which areas of concern you'll eliminate.

g. To help determine your landing page strategy you should sort the areas of concern for each Ad Group you'll be using from highest to lowest. Depending on the priority (i.e. message) of each Adgroup (i.e. the keywords and key phrases) your landing page's sales copy should be written to grab your prospects' attention accordingly.

h. When writing the sales copy for each of your landing pages, or any follow up correspondence, read through the responses of the survey respondents. If you sorted these responses by category and/or difficulty you can further segment your target groups and modify the copy to appeal more directly by addressing their concerns specifically and using the same language as the respondent has used.

> "I don't know the rules of grammar... If you're trying
> to persuade people to do something, or buy something, it
> seems to me you should use their language, the language
> they use every day, the language in which they think. We
> try to write in the vernacular."
>
> David Ogilvy

There are very subtle differences in language that can make the difference between buyer and non-buyer. The secret is to de-code the language used in the surveys to decipher exactly what the market really wants.

i. Talk to any prospects that leave contact information, whether it is by email or telephone. Try to run telephone focus groups or individual phone interviews or face-to-face interviews for each and every segment.

5. DESIGN LANDING PAGES

It's vital to base your landing page designs and sales copy on the *Keyword Continuum*™. The *Keyword Continuum*™ determines that you should use the same keyword or key phrase that the prospect originally searched for, or clicked on, throughout your website's whole click-through path, search funnel, or sales funnel (i.e. Keyword or key phrase > PPC ad > Landing Page > Pay Page > Follow Up etc.). This content should be supplemented by using the research data from online surveys to totally engage the reader.

The design of your website will depend on what you are selling; if you have a shop with multiple products then you will probably use an online shopping cart with multiple pages. If you are selling services you might decide to use a corporate-looking website with plenty of credibility-building background information over multiple pages. However, for one-off products and services a one page website might be a more effective option.

ONE PAGE WEBSITES

Research has shown that for lead-generation, surveys, low ticket items or impulse buys, one page websites are usually more productive. The fact is that with every invitation to click a high percentage of prospects are lost. The psychological reasons for this are many and varied but most researchers seem to think that it is due to our 'I've started, so I'll finish' attitude. However, when asked to click to another page, we mentally say 'I don't want to start another task' and leave.

Some research also suggests that some susceptible prospects see the invitation to click away as an opportunity to leave the pressure of the sales pitch and break the hypnotic sales trance they may be experiencing – something the one page sell doesn't allow.

Note: I've written several books and articles on multiple page website design, and you can learn a great deal about the subject by visiting www.riskeliminator.com; however, here I'd like to concentrate on the use of one page websites.

HOW TO CREATE A ONE PAGE WEBSITES

A one page website (also known as 'one page sales letter websites' or 'mini websites') is used to 'hard sell' a product. Because most people don't actually read anything online; they scan a page, seeking out info that is bold, in a larger font size, in a different color, or in a bulleted format; Internet marketers use one page websites to highlight the most important information about their product to catch the reader's eye as they scan the page.

To develop a one page website you'll need to do the following:

1. A niche target market. You need to be able to identify and know something about a very specific niche market before proceeding to the next step.

2. A product. Ideally, suited to your chosen niche market e.g. an e-book, an e-course, or a set of DVDs for a 'How to' course.

3. A domain name. The domain name should reflect your product's purpose or benefit, your product's name, or a prominent feature of your product. For example, if you are selling an e-course on underwater photography you should get a domain name like underwaterphotographycourse.com. Try and purchase the '.com' version of the domain name, or the hyphenated version of the .com domain name.

4. Added value (i.e. a 'give-away'). The purpose of your website is (i) to convert each visitor into a paying customer, or (ii) get the contact info of your visitors and convert them into a paying customer later through follow up contact. The best way

to obtain contact info from a visitor is to create a related information product (e.g. e-book, electronic tips booklet, special report, podcast or other audio file, e-course, video, etc.) in which the content is so compelling that the visitor provides their name and email address to obtain the free giveaway.

5. The sales page. The formula for a one page sales letter website is generally an attention-getting headline, a strong opening statement, body of the sales copy that outlines the features and benefits of what you're offering, the actual offer itself, testimonials of others who've used the product, and then asking for the sale.

6. You will also need a merchant account, shopping cart software, auto-responders (automated email program) so you can automatically follow up with your buyers, and an email broadcast function so that you can send out special notices to the customers or prospects on your list.

Note: You can educate your prospects about any other offers you may have on separate sales pages or in any follow-up dialogue (through auto-responders etc.) and offer them a choice of products or services targeted specifically at their segment.

You'll Make $ERIOUS
MONEY Online!

PART TWO

DON'T RE-INVENT THE WHEEL!

Chapter Five

If It Don't Fit, Don't Force It

THE TEN CHARACTERISTICS OF ALL SUCCESSFUL ONLINE BUSINESSES

These are the 10 basic characteristics that all successful websites have:

1. Appeals to a narrowly defined/targeted audience
2. Provides a genuinely useful/desirable product or service
3. Establishes a buyer-seller relationship and customer loyalty
4. Uses technology judiciously (e.g. relevant, appropriate, efficient and simple to use)
5. Focuses on customer's convenience (e.g. is user friendly)
6. Provides an exclusive, bespoke or specialized product or service
7. Saves the customer money
8. Provides products or services difficult to acquire elsewhere (e.g. offline)
9. Adds value; provides info about products or services, provides more than competitors, is entertaining, makes purchasing more pleasurable etc.
10. Has structures in place to cope with any potential demand (e.g. payment and delivery systems)

The *Strategic Fit Matrix*™ overleaf examines 10 different companies with a successful online product. Given the evidence, it would seem that a score of 7 ½ or above would indicate a good chance of success online.

Strategic Fit Matrix (0 = poor strategic fit; ½ = partial strategic fit; 1 = good strategic fit)

Checklist	Spread Shirt	Hungry Pod	Positives Dating	Kanda Systems	Book Swim	Race Wax	Antenna Balls	Card Stix	Moms on Edge	Merrick Mints
Appeals to Internet audience	1	1	½	½	1	½	½	½	½	½
Provides a genuinely valuable or useful product or service	1	1	1	1	1	1	1	1	1	1
Establishes a buyer-seller relationship & trust	1	1	1	½	1	1	½	½	1	1
Uses technology judiciously	1	1	1	1	1	1	1	1	1	1
Focuses on customer's convenience	1	1	1	½	1	1	1	1	1	1
Provides an exclusive, bespoke or specialized product or service	1	1	1	1	0	1	1	1	1	1
Saves the customer money	½	0	0	½	1	½	0	1	0	½
Provides products or services difficult to acquire elsewhere	1	1	1	1	0	1	1	1	0	1
Adds value; provides info about products or services; is entertaining or makes purchasing more pleasurable	½	0	1	½	1	½	1	½	1	1
Has structures in place to cope with any potential demand	1	1	1	1	1	1	1	1	1	1
Score (out of 10)	**9**	**8**	**8½**	**7 ½**	**8**	**8½**	**8**	**8 ½**	**7½**	**9**

"Risk comes from not knowing what you're doing."
Warren Buffet

Chapter Six

The Sincerest Form of Flattery

SUCCESSFUL CASE STUDIES

The purpose of using actual case studies is to illustrate which businesses have the correct *Strategic Fit™* for e-commerce. The following list of small businesses represents a wide spectrum of commerce: retail, service, manufacturing, entertainment and leisure sectors. Using the *Strategic Fit Matrix™* you can predict or confirm whether each company should be successful online.

The ten case studies are:

1.	Antenna Balls	promotions
2.	Book Swim	book sales
3.	Card Stix	greeting cards
4.	Hungry Pod	music services
5.	Kanda Systems	electronic sales
6.	Moms on Edge	parenting
7.	Positives Dating	dating/relationships
8.	Racewax.com	sporting goods
9.	Spreadshirt.com	clothing
10.	The Merrick Mint	coins

ANTENNA BALLS

Since 1998, *Antenna Balls* (www.antennaballs.com) has been topping car antennas with happy faces, 8-balls and even cowgirls—complete with braids and hats. Jason Wall is President and CEO of In-Concept Inc., the company behind Antennaballs.com, which manufactures more than 500,000 custom antenna balls per month.

PLATE 20: ANTENNA BALLS WEBSITE

In mid-1997, Wall saw a television commercial about the franchise *Jack In The Box* claiming that the company had sold more than 3 million antenna balls. Sensing an opportunity, Wall came up with a few designs he thought would penetrate the auto accessory and novelty industries. The designs stuck.

After selling four million balls through local gas stations and convenience stores in 2004 and 2005, Wall landed some major national accounts, including AutoZone, Circle K and Wal-Mart. HappyBalls.com, online retailer of antenna ball toppers, and In-Concept, Inc., (www.antennaballs.com), developer and distributor of custom antenna toppers, announced an agreement to join forces in January of 2006. Their website now carries over 500 unique and collectible antenna toppers, making the company one of the largest antenna ball manufacturing and distribution companies in the United States.

Antenna Balls is a great example of a small company that capitalized on a brand new product and profitable niche with a great marketing idea. They offer their customers a way to get their message out in the public eye through a viral marketing platform. Their competitive advantage over their competitors is the wide variety of balls available and their ability to provide specific customization, backed up by an extensive distribution network.

BOOK SWIM

Book Swim (www.bookswim.com) provides a nationwide book rental service, from new releases to classics, bestsellers and children's books. Subscription plans start at under $15 per month and allow as many as 11 books to be borrowed at a time with no late fees or shipping fees. Members can even buy the books if they choose.

College friends George Burke and Shamoon Siddiqui spent a lot of time in bookstores reading books but not buying them - so the idea was born. In 2006, they launched Book Swim using personal savings and book donations. By April 2007, they had their first customer.

PLATE 21: BOOKSWIM WEBSITE

The 20+ employee company currently offers 200,000 book titles but uses a JIT (just-in-time) inventory model, which allows them to keep costs low. Most inventory comes from distributors but, as volume increases, publishers have begun to approach them directly. Since launching Book Swim, the pair has greatly increased the number of books they purchase daily, and company growth is more than tripling monthly with a projected 2009 year end sales of $800,000.

In addition to a convenient way to receive books, Book Swim is also promoted as a "green" company. Book Swim encourages book rental, rather than purchasing new books, in part to help reduce the number of trees cut down every year for American book production. Additionally, for every gift card sold they plant a tree through a partnership with *EcoLibris*.

Renting also saves readers money. By the time Book Swim reaches its target of a million books in circulation by 2010, its founders would have saved subscribers USD 22,070,000 over list price!

Book Swim used an already proven model and applied it to a new niche. Although the idea of free books has been around in libraries for years, (hence the two "0" scores on the *Strategic Fit Matrix*™), Book Swim has found a unique way to market their idea to their customers, thus making it a successful online venture.

CARD STIX

Card Stix Inc (www.cardstixcollection.com) started in late 2006 producing a unique style of greeting card. Card Stix Inc. makes greeting card stickers that adhere to birthday presents, wine bottles, hostess gifts and wedding favors. Erica Peale and Meredith Kole, friends since college, lamented the high cost of buying numerous birthday cards that got torn off packages or were sent to toddlers who couldn't read. Thus, Card Stix was born. They are sold on the company website and in 200 stores nationwide. Meredith and Erica also offer an up-sell, allowing customers to have their card stix personalized.

An initial investment of $18,000 was used for a website and their first stickers printed through a Maine printing company. Currently, the company is run entirely by the two, with Meredith creating the designs and greeting card messages, and Erica doing the marketing. In 2007, the company grossed $30,000 but they put all the profit back into the company.

In addition to selling through retail stores and their online stores Card Stix offers opportunities for others to get in on the action. Using a marketing platform made famous by Tupperware and used now for a myriad of products, Card Stix offers home parties with 15% of the sales going to the hostess. Card Stix has also capitalized on the "Avon" platform, allowing people to sell the products through a "Look Book" and earn a 15% commission.

PLATE 22: CARDSTIX WEBSITE

The challenge for Card Stix is to help customers understand that their product is different from traditional gift labels that are smaller and don't contain a message beyond "To" and "From." One of the main advantages is that Card Stix are 33 percent cheaper than a traditional greetings card.

Having a product that appeals to the online audience, and is such a specialized product that saves the customer money, as well as a website that is easy to navigate, all helps Card Stix score so well on the *Strategic Fit Matrix™*.

HUNGRY POD

Hungry Pod's (www.hungrypod.com) owner, Catherine Keane, made over $100,000 a year uploading music to other people's iPods in her first year of business. Started in September of 2004, the idea came to her when an acquaintance offered her $500 to load his CD collection onto his iPod.

Most of her customers are busy professionals in their 20s and 30s with disposable income and demographics matching those outlined in the *Strategic Fit Matrix™*, and as annual sales increased, so did her staff, adding more employees and a marketing specialist.

Originally, the service converted CDs to MP3 format and loaded them into an iPod or any other digital music player. This service began by helping 30 or so clients in her area. When she realized how quickly her sales were growing, she hired a web designer and took her concept online.

Keane thought out some added value extras to up-sell, including DVD backup and a personal music shopper. Keane is a music consultant and, for a fee, would recommend similar artists based on a customer's current tastes, and purchase CDs from an online music service for the customer.

PLATE 23: HUNGRYPOD WEBSITE

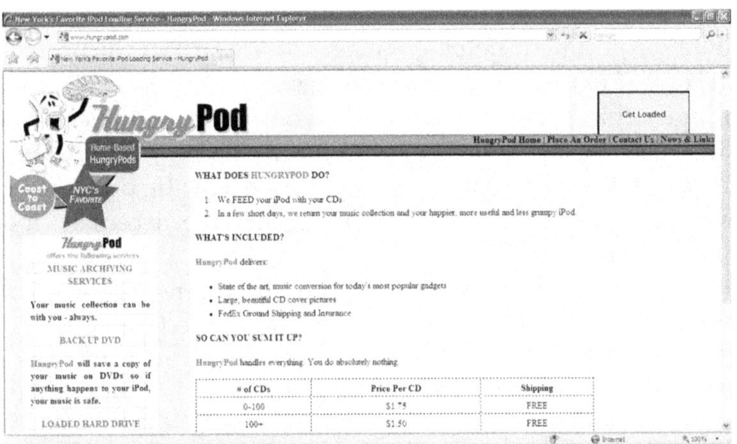

# of CDs	Price Per CD	Shipping
0-100	$1.75	FREE
100+	$1.50	FREE

Hungry Pod is a good example of identifying a problem and creating a solution to address that problem. When Hungry Pod got started, there were no other businesses offering the service, thus giving the company first-mover advantage (and, consequently, a high rating in several areas of the *Strategic Fit Matrix*™). The company's products don't necessarily save customers any money but it does save them time, and for busy professionals time is often a more valuable commodity.

Entrepreneurs often forget that decisions made on day one can have huge implications down the road. As Hungry Pod understands, it's not enough to build a business worth a fortune; you have to make sure you have an 'exit' strategy; a way to get the money back out. Acquisition is one of the most common exit strategies and in May of 2008, Moondog Digital, which also provides music-loading solutions, acquired Hungry Pod. Hungry Pod is an example of an entrepreneur that has gone through the ideal lifecycle of a successful business – idea, start up, success, sell for profit, and retire rich!

KANDA SYSTEMS

Kanda Systems Limited (www.kanda.com), founded in 1994, is an independent company run by two former college lecturers. The company specializes in assisting organizations with the rapid development of applications for microelectronics. Kanda's equipment helps engineers work on the silicon chips that control various electronic devices.

Engineers, particularly in the computer and electronics industries, use the Internet extensively to research completed designs that can be adapted for their own specific purpose and develop or adapt chip designs or acquire the necessary tools for the job.

Since the firm has been trading on the Internet it has grown from a two-man firm operating from a shed to a leading company in its field worldwide. It now turns over millions of dollars and exports 95 per cent its products. The company has a comprehensive range of development tools, training programs and associated products backed by a support team focused on addressing the needs of their customers at all levels of technical ability.

The company's competitive advantage has been its dedicated manufacturing research and development facility that enables it to take products from the drawing board to delivery in the shortest time possible.

PLATE 24: KANDA SYSTEMS WEBSITE

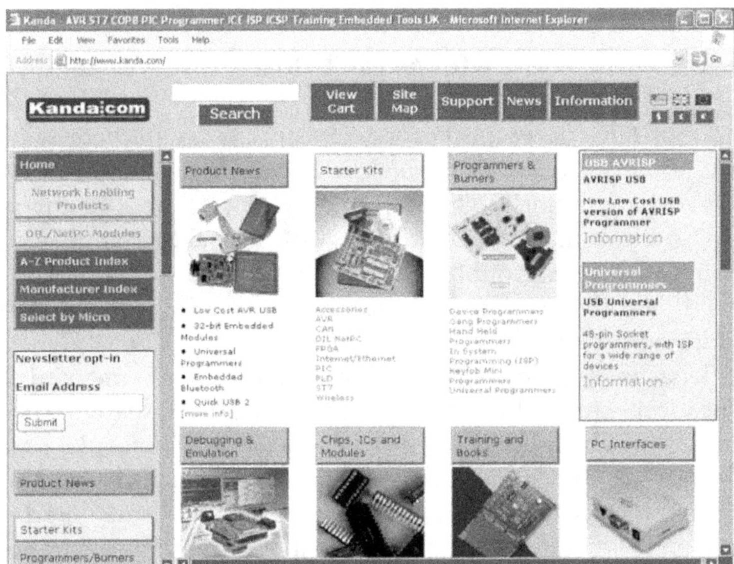

In addition, the company also undertakes bespoke programming and design consultancy projects on behalf of its customers. Users can also take advantage of Kanda's comprehensive range of complete training packages such as starter kits, which makes it possible for even the smallest of developers to extend their portfolio of skills and services into an area previously prohibited by cost.

Kanda Systems Ltd. is an excellent example of how a small business, providing a specialized, genuinely useful product which is difficult to acquire elsewhere, to a niche market, can be extremely successful online. Kanda proves that by establishing a buyer-seller relationship through providing information about their products, a small firm can achieve consistent, repeat orders. Kanda also has the dependable back-end structures in place. It uses a parcel courier delivery service and its products are available internationally through major distributors and catalogue-based organizations to cope with any potential demand. This case study also illustrates the potential for small firms to be successful online by supplying other firms (i.e. B2B).

MOMS ON EDGE

Moms on Edge (www.momsonedge.com) is a complete work-from-home concept. Elena Neitlich and Cari Whiddon were two working moms in Florida. As good friends and neighbors, they hit upon the idea of starting Moms on Edge while going through the usual trouble of bringing up children who fell out of bed, wet themselves, had tantrums while eating, and other childhood problems.

Elena is a Fine Arts graduate, while Cari majored in Education. This helped them with the initial research. These two women have developed a line of educational, play, and childcare products that include time-out mats, 'potty training' devices, blocks, dice, and mats that discipline and entertain children. They have bath products such as tear free shampoo, gentle creams, and bubble bath. Recently a collection of bath and beauty products for mothers who don't have a lot of time has been launched.

Moms on Edge started off carefully, combining their website with an eBay shop and an open offer to wholesalers. Andrew and Elena Neitlich write SEO articles, and all four partners blog actively to publicize their products.

PLATE 25: MOMS ON EDGE WEBSITE

Moms on Edge have a colorful and friendly website. Although there are some lingering problems with managing the manufacturing and procuring of products, Moms on Edge has captured a niche market of busy mothers who want ready solutions that they can buy online with convenient payment methods. This business passes the *Strategic Fit Matrix*™ test and has excellent prospects.

POSITIVES DATING

As with most dating websites, this business model has an excellent *Strategic Fit*™ for the Internet. However, www.positivesdating.com is also an excellent example of identifying and exploiting a profitable niche as a segment within an already established online industry.

The success of *Positives Dating* relies on the existence of a sufficient number of target market customers existing online and those potential customers wanting to contact similar people; the power of 'network effects' (see PART THREE: THE GOLDEN SECRETS OF BUSINESS SUCCESS).

Positives Dating offers a powerful social networking and dating service for the HIV positive community, allowing subscribers to place personal dating advertisements. Members search the database looking for casual or long-term relationships with other HIV positive people. They are from all ages and walks of life and hail from the US, Canada, Europe and Asia. The website's revenue is derived from subscription fees.

PLATE 26: POSITIVES DATING WEBSITE

With over one million AIDS/HIV positive people in the US, college students Paul Graves and Brandon Koechlin recognized the opportunity after attending a sociology seminar on AIDS. There they became aware of the huge problem infected people faced in establishing romantic relationships or networking socially.

The partners borrowed $50,000 and created an online forum for HIV positive people. The website became operational in January 2005 to instant success, closing the year with 2,500 members and $60,000 in revenue. It today has about 50,000 members with healthy sales.

The biggest hurdle is encouraging online AIDs carriers to divulge their information in such a public way. Although Positives Dating assures its users of the safeguards used to protect their personal information, the stigma attached to the disease makes online users wary, thus the lower score on the *Strategic Fit Matrix*™ for appealing to an Internet audience. The service doesn't save its customers money compared to other online dating websites, but the company's domination of this profitable niche makes this less of a negative factor.

Positives Dating certainly meets the criteria of a successful online business.

RACE WAX

Racewax.com (www.racewax.com) as the name makes clear, deals with waxes that enhance the speed of skis and snowboards. It was born as a family business in 1999 and ten years down the line it maintains its personable charm. Started off in the early days of the Internet by a small town American family, it is now looked upon as one of the most revered sporting goods companies on the web.

Dr. Marc and Emelda Desrosiers were parents trying to buy skiing equipments for son Christian. Dr. Desrosiers, a PhD chemist, realized that wax coats could be developed at a cheaper price than the ones available in main street shops. It was entrepreneurial thinking that convinced him that business success could be 'achieved through technology, not manpower'. So Racewax.com was developed exclusively with an Internet-based clientele in mind.

Racewax.com is an example of successful market capture by targeting a very limited demographic with a highly specialized product. Marc has promoted himself as 'Dr. D' and advises racers on technology, waxes, brushes, scrapping, applying, and developing their own racing wax on his website, blog, and forum as well as in online racing communities.

PLATE 27: RACE WAX WEBSITE

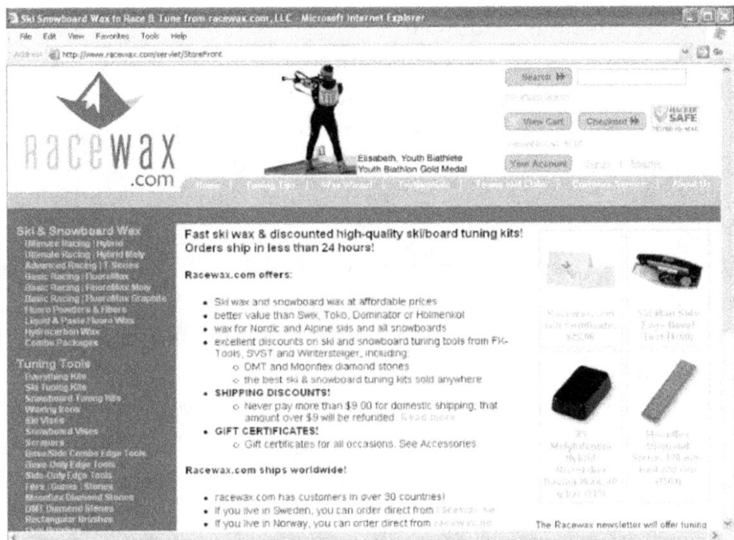

The Racewax.com product range includes, apart from waxes, brushes, caps, t-shirts, stickers, scrapers and other related skate board tuning tools. The customer may pay using various cards, and shipping within North America and Canada is free. The flavor of the website is remarkably friendly; with a direct, no-frills design. This tone suits the target customer absolutely, as witnessed by the many testimonials. Racewax.com scores deservingly high on the *Strategic Fit Matrix*™, as it meets all the requirements for succeeding on the web.

SPREADSHIRT

SpreadShirt (www.spreadshirt.com) started in 2002 in Leipzig, Germany, by business school students Lukasz Gadowski and Matthias Spiess, as a desktop venture. The company won the Futuresax Award in 2002, the HP Business Innovation Award in 2004, and a special German Internet award as a promising company in 2005, and is now a part of the Europe Fortune 500.

A classic example of how innovative young people can become e-millionaires, Spreadshirt today has 230 employees globally, several branches and a plush 1,000 square meter office space as its headquarters.

Spreadshirt's success stems from product choice, creativity, and marketing. The most important business strategy was to offer clients 'Spreadshops' (i.e. helping anyone who is interested in opening a free website for vending white labeled Spreadshirt products with their own designs, while both parties earn commissions).

Currently, Spreadshirt has some 300,000 Internet shop partners. This includes big brands such as Samsung, Coca Cola, Chuck Norris, and The Guardian Newspaper apart from artists and students.

Spreadshirt manufactures several varieties of tee shirts, sweatshirts, jackets, aprons, mugs, caps, bags, underwear, and shoes. It prints designs for both customers and prospective partners. Spreadshirt helps its partners with setting up their Internet shops, procuring the products, printing designs, shipping, and web marketing.

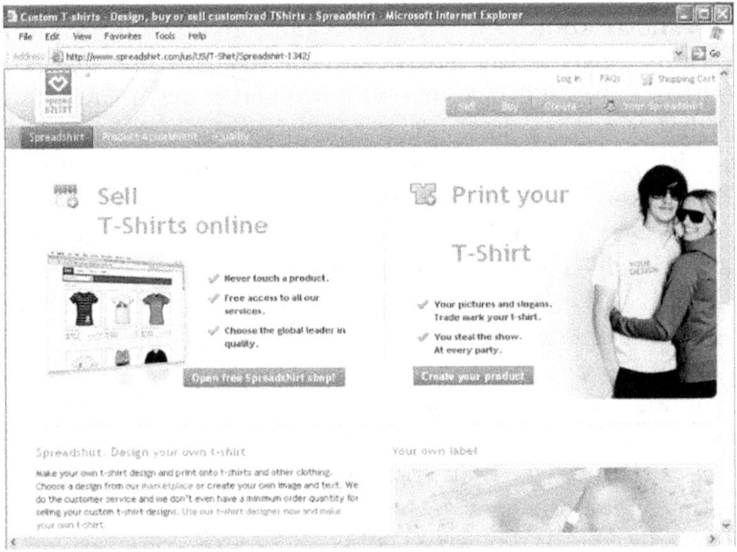

The company has a sound understanding of e-business and marketing, with its own forum, blog, and a chat room for partners as well as publishing regular publicity articles and press releases. Its web pages are optimized for search engines, and the landing pages from PPC advertisements are relevant to the keyword searched for in a search engine (e.g. Google, MSN etc.). The products are target market-friendly (youth orientated) and perfectly suit heavy users of the Internet.

Future growth prospects are very bright by all predictions for the company, which has seen a heavy inflow of venture capital. Spreadshirt has been able to combine creativity and technology in a way that suits e-commerce best, and scores highest in the *Strategic Fit Matrix*™.

THE MERRICK MINT

Established in the late 1980s, *The Merrick Mint* (www.merrickmint.com) is a private limited company that currently tops the US market for colorized coins. It sells its products through multiple distribution channels, including its website, retail outlets, television shopping channels and specialty stores, including wholesalers, promotional networks and collectors' clubs and websites.

The Merrick Mint holds a license to sell colorized coins but also sells gold trading cards, sports cards, and candy novelties. They also sell educational products such as DIY trading card stickers for children above eight years of age, of which they produce over one thousand varieties annually.

Founders Darryl and Matthew Abromowitz have flourished by maintaining a fine balance of flexibility and exclusivity when it comes to their products. Starting with servicing vending machines, they went on to sell sports cards, licensed gold trading cards, colorized coins and sports coins, as well as candy novelties, which was awarded best product in the 2005 Chicago Candy Show.

PLATE 29: THE MERRICK MINT WEBSITE

Their Internet strategy has been well thought out, since buyers of memorabilia were already familiar with their name. When customers got the chance to buy directly from the company instead of eBay auctions, The Merrick Mint saw a sudden growth in revenues.

The company has successfully combined the advantages of a global pre-existence with that of targeting and capturing a niche market on the web. An online catalogue, a well maintained mailing list, and the chance to pay conveniently in multiple ways has helped the company to make good profits online. Their website is easy to use and has detailed photographs of all products. The Merrick Mint's online presence has nearly all of the assets required for a perfect *Strategic Fit*™.

You'll Make $ERIOUS
MONEY Online!

Chapter Seven

To Make Money, Go Where the Money Is

WHERE ARE THE MONEY-MAKING OPPORTUNITIES ONLINE?

The size of the Internet presents huge opportunities for almost any business with the correct *Strategic Fit*™ for e-commerce. Let's look at the types of business opportunities that are available online.

There are two main types of e-commerce; B2B (business to business) and B2C (business to consumer). B2B means that your business has other businesses as customers. For instance, you create advertising graphics for other businesses. B2C means that individual consumers are your customer. For instance, you sell underwater cameras to diving enthusiasts. Sometimes the line is not so clearly drawn. For instance, SpreadShirt is both a B2B and B2C company. Their end user can be a person or a company.

First, let's take a look at some successful B2B Internet-based business ideas:

BROKERING

Brokering of anything on the Internet would appear to be a good business opportunity. Typically, the broker does not have any stock, does not own the merchandise, and the transaction is made between the selling and buying parties. The broker facilitates the deal, acts as a consultant for both parties, and takes care of the possible paperwork.

For instance, online ticket brokering is the resale of tickets for sold-out events. Prices are determined by demand and/or availability and are not fixed, distinguishing it from purchasing tickets directly from a venue, retailer or official seller. Customers generally approach online ticket brokers when these primary sellers are unable to supply tickets.

Several different brokering opportunities exist in travel, insurance, real estate, tickets, and trading. In fact, if you have access to a product that others want, being the go-between is an excellent online opportunity.

CONSULTING

A consultant is an expert or a professional in a specific field who has a deep and wide knowledge of the subject matter. Often a consultant provides expertise to clients who require a particular type of knowledge or service for a specific period of time. In other situations, companies implementing a major project may need additional experienced staff to assist with increased work during that period.

PLATE 30: E-COMMERCE CONSULTANT WEBSITE

You should have at least a good level of knowledge on a particular topic. If you don't have first-hand experience, you can partner with professionals who can help you.

There are thousands of companies offering consultancy services of every kind over the Internet. Though the most successful were once Internet-related, such as web masters, now consultants span a huge range of sectors. Such sectors include creating and maintaining auction websites, project planners, think tanks, automation, inventory control, home business, business recovery, expense reduction, merger and acquisition, business plans, franchise opportunities, offshore business registration, and many more.

A powerful, yet relatively simple promotional idea for this business is to publish a newsletter or blog. You may also, for example, want to form a 'society' or 'association' for the specific field of expertise (e.g. National Association of E-Commerce Consultants).

FREELANCE SERVICES

According to the US Department of Labor, Bureau of Labor Statistics, approximately 10.3 million workers in the US are independent contractors. That is 7.4% of the US workforce. And in the past three years, companies have increased their outsourcing by 22% on the Internet, making freelancing a great B2B opportunity.

Essentially, most jobs that you do can be freelanced. For instance, you could be an accountant/bookkeeper, appraiser, computer programmer, corporate event planner, data entry/processor, editor/copyeditor, financial planner, grant writer, sales/marketing consultant, web designer, writer, etc., etc.

PLATE 31: FREELANCE COPYWRITER WEBSITE

Businesses choose to work with freelancers when they require certain skills only at certain times. For instance, a certain project may need a writer but hiring a writer full-time would be a waste of resources. For most companies, hiring a freelancer is economical since the business does not have to pay for insurance, retirement, or sick leave.

If you are a freelancer, you really need to promote yourself as being an expert in your field of expertise. This presence is what builds credibility and is acquired by marketing your services in an appropriate and effective manner.

One way to gain that presence is to go through a freelance service such as Elance (www.elance.com). Websites such as this help those with business projects to get in touch with freelancers who have the skills to complete those projects.

PLATE 32: ELANCE WEBSITE

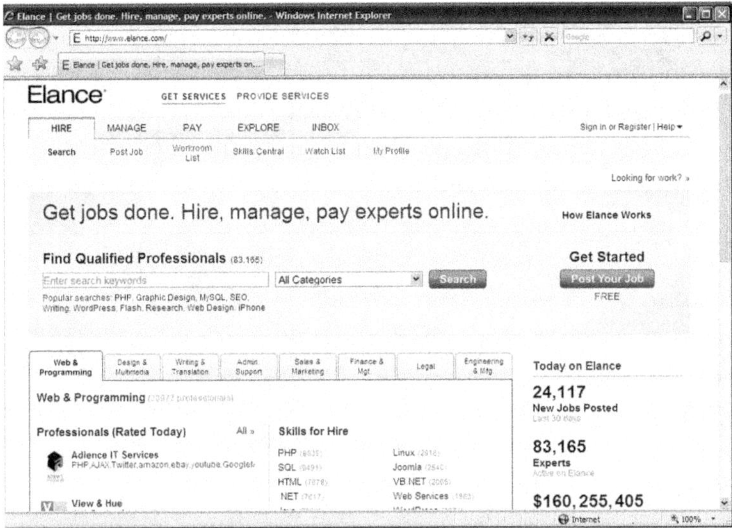

Although this service requires you to pay a service fee based on bid amounts as well as a monthly user's fee, it is a good way to secure regular work and gain a positive reputation in your field of expertise.

INFORMATION

The advent of the Internet has made 24-hour access to information and databases a high-demand resource. Gathering these information aggregates and adding services to them is now the business of companies like the Thomas Register of Manufacturers that can bring a base of information from the print medium to the Internet. Or, alternatively, you could gather, organize, and link to new information and services on the Internet without ever using printed materials. Such websites are known as information websites or "infomediaries".

PLATE 33: THOMAS REGISTER WEBSITE

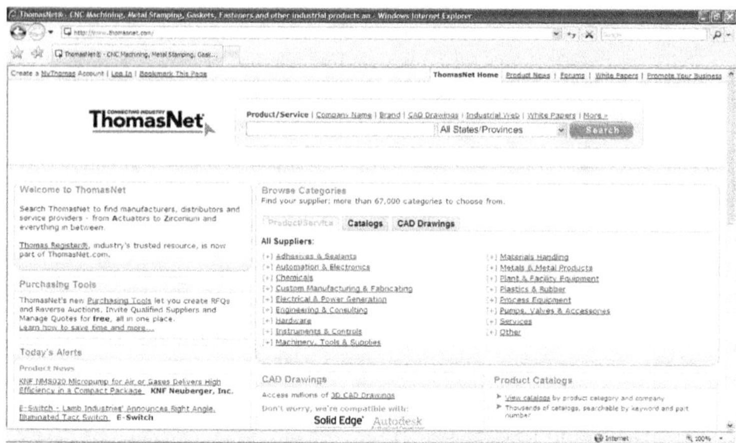

For knowledge-based services providing some advice, such as updates, may be offered free but any in-depth or specific advice should be charged for.

Infomediaries are the middlemen between marketers and consumers whose purpose is to facilitate better marketing matches. Consumers disclose their personal preferences to an infomediary, who can then offer marketers the ability to engage in highly targeted marketing campaigns. Infomediaries can also use their aggregated consumer demand to make consumer-favorable deals with marketers.

Any promotional material used to advertise such services should include credibility-building devices, resumes (CVs), client testimonials, and any relevant articles etc. and be targeted at the right audience. Information-based businesses such as these can make excellent revenue when targeted at specific industries requiring specific, detailed 'inside' information.

INTERNET RESEARCH BUSINESS

With the vast amount of information provided on the Internet, wading through countless websites to find what you are searching for can become a tedious task. Those who are able to narrow down their searches on topics of interest can start their own home-based Internet research business.

In many cases of Internet-based research it is necessary to be a specialist in one field. However, you can add closely-related content to your field of specialty to the research. In order for an individual to find pertinent Internet-based information, you have to know precisely where to look for that information.

The market for Internet researchers is very large (not surprisingly, as the average B2B sales transaction exceeds $80,000). Research services range from sales leads to candidate sourcing and everything in between. Almost any company will pay $5,000 to $20,000 for information that can help them earn an additional $50,000 to $100,000, faster and easier.

PRODUCT SUPPLY AND PROCUREMENT EXCHANGES

E-procurement (sometimes also known as 'supplier exchange') is the business-to-business purchase and sale of supplies and services through the Internet. Typically, e-procurement websites allow qualified and registered users to look for buyers or sellers of goods and services. Depending on the approach, buyers or sellers may specify costs or invite bids. Transactions can be initiated and completed online. For ongoing purchases you can qualify customers for volume discounts or special offers.

The advantage to the customer includes getting the right product, from the right supplier, at the right time, for the right price and the right quantity. E-procurement has the advantage of taking supply chain management to the next level; providing real time information to the vendor about the customer's needs. For example, a vendor may have an agreement with a customer to automatically ship materials when the customer's stock level reaches a low point, thus by-passing the need for the customer to repeatedly request it – thus reducing time, inventory costs and transaction costs.

RECRUITING

Finding quality employees, especially to fill executive level corporate positions, is not always an easy task. Most Human Resource departments simply don't have the resources available to screen, filter and find qualified executives. A recruiting business will provide executive search, screening and pre-interview services. Money is earned by charging a finder fee, typically a percentage of first year salary.

PLATE 34: THOMAS REGISTER WEBSITE

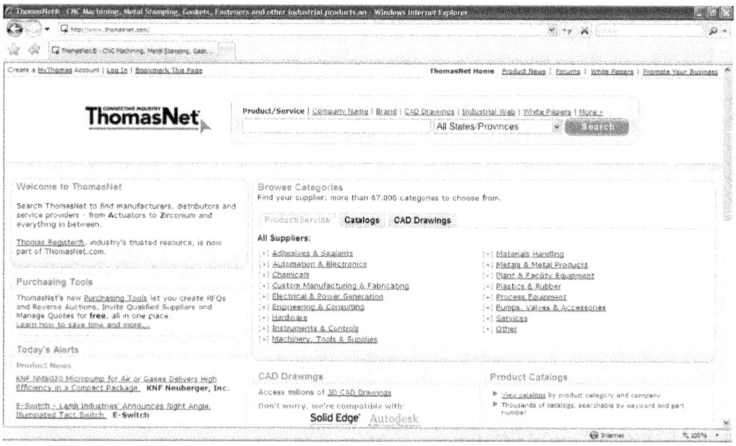

Establishing a network of qualified executive candidates can be the big key to a successful venture. Therefore, networking with those "in the know" such as those in Human Resources, is essential. Establishing a recruiting niche by focusing on key industries (software, pharmaceuticals, etc.) or functional specialties (finance, sales, etc.) will lead to a greater chance of success.

You can provide further services by representing executive clients in their corporate job search or leverage your business experience and offer coaching services to executives in areas such as public speaking, negotiations, conflict resolution and employee motivation.

VIRTUAL ASSISTANT

Although a Virtual Assistant (VA) is a form of freelancer, it is included here because this service has seen such a huge demand online. A VA is an independent person who works closely with a limited number of clients from home, communicating via the Internet, phone, fax etc.

PLATE 35: VIRTUAL ASSISTANT WEBSITE

A VA uses administrative skills such as bookkeeping, desktop publishing, research, meeting and travel planning, project management and public relations. Most VAs form a long-term partnership with a few clients, thus giving them even more added value as they learn their client's specific business needs. Clients can be located anywhere in the world, so this is a geographically limitless opportunity.

To be a VA, you need to be comfortable with computer programs and have strong word processing, spreadsheet and secretarial skills. You can also specialize in specific areas or industries such as translation, Internet marketing, real estate, web design and desktop publishing. Opportunities for VAs are expanding as companies outsource support staff. And, as more small businesses grow, they may need support but not be able to afford in-house staffing.

Now let's look at some successful B2C Internet-based business ideas.

ART PRINTS

Many artists focus completely on their art and fail to consider how they will market their creations. Understanding this need provides you with a niche opportunity. You could develop a website that features art prints. The website can be indexed by the theme of the prints. The more specialized the theme, the more likely you are to be successful, provided it is a popular niche.

PLATE 36: ART PRINTS WEBSITE

Artists from around the world can submit pictures of their prints. Upon sale of a print the artist would ship it to the purchaser and you and the artist would receive a percentage of the sales value. Ideally, marketing efforts would be aimed at individuals and organizations that routinely purchase art prints such as decorators, interior designers, corporations, and property developers. Depending on the niche you specialize in, you may well find that individual collectors are also a significant market.

But don't feel the need to stop at prints. Following the same technique, you could sell artists' 3D creations, such as sculptures, using photos of their works. This type of venture is easy to establish and could be operated from home on a part-time basis.

AUCTIONS

Online auctions, such as eBay (www.ebay.com), where companies sell their stock to the highest bidder, are very popular on the Internet. Online auctions such as these are particularly popular with the young and/or affluent Internet audience. There is an increasing amount of niche, specialized auction websites appearing. As always, the key is finding an under-serviced, profitable niche market to sell it to.

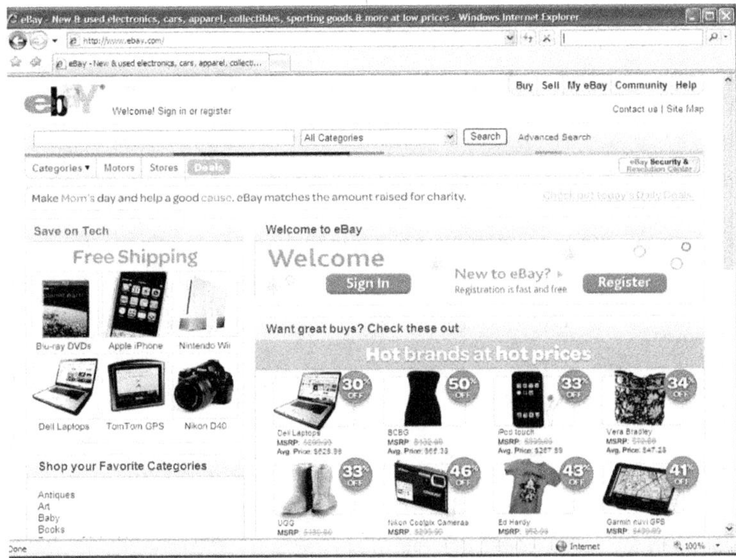

The challenge will be to develop a compelling advertisement campaign to convince your target customers that using your services will save them time and hassle in the online auction and fulfillment process.

BLOGGING

Blogs are online 'logs' or diaries kept by enthusiasts or businesses for people interested in the subject of the blog. Blogging is the term used for maintaining or contributing to a blog. The most common way bloggers can earn money from blogging is via advertising programs such as Google's Ad Sense, Chitika's eMiniMalls, WidgetBucks and Text Link Ads etc.

Bloggers also use RSS advertising, sponsorship, advertising directly on blogs, as well as some bloggers being paid to write on certain topics by companies. Affiliate Programs, such as Amazon, Linkshare, Clickbank and Commission Junction, as well as thousands of other affiliate schemes, are also a good form of revenue. Bloggers can also make money from selling digital assets, e-books, courses and tele-seminars.

PLATE 38: BLOGGERS FOR HIRE WEBSITE

As businesses continue to use blogs as marketing and SEO tools, there is an increasing demand for bloggers to maintain company blogs. Many of these companies have internal staff to take on blogging duties, but an increasing number of them are hiring specialist bloggers to run their blogs. Bloggers for Hire (www.bloggersforhire.com) is worth looking at if you're looking for this type of work.

BOOK SALES

Books sell well on the Internet because they are comparatively inexpensive and customers know what they are going to get for their money. However, your company's website does not need to be a bookseller in order to sell them. Several of the big web booksellers offer affiliate or "partnership" programs for other websites where a company provides an ordering button on its website linked to a publisher's website containing books relevant to whatever the company's website is promoting. The publisher then handles all the order processing and fulfillment, and pays a percentage of the cover price as a commission.

PLATE 39: BOOK RETAILER WEBSITE

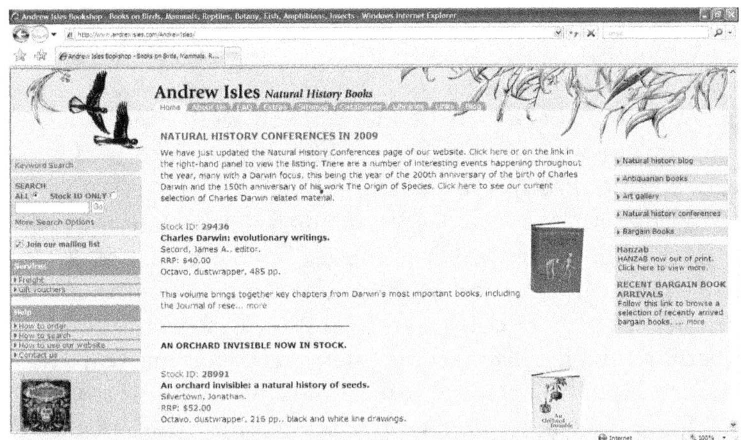

The publisher handles all customer questions and requests (including cancellations and returns) and then packages and ships any book order anywhere in the world. Your company then sends the bill to the customer, collects the cash, and hands over a portion of the fee to the publisher. Other companies, such as Amazon (www.amazon.com), offer similar schemes.

There is no reason why owner-managers of small businesses should not make a success of book selling online, providing they identify a niche market to target. Obscure or specialist books can be difficult to acquire and take weeks to be delivered. This fact provides an opportunity for specialist bookshops.

CHARGING FOR ACCESS

If your company's website contains valuable content you can password-protect part of its website and charge a fee to access that information. Large corporations, learning institutions and researchers are constantly requiring up-to-date, often obscure research or intelligence. These customers are used to paying large fees for high quality data or information.

92

COLLECTABLES

There is a large and growing market for collectables on the Net. Small niche businesses, as well as individuals, are using the huge global web network to reach a far larger percentage of interested customers. Antiques, as specialized goods appealing to a specific niche market, sell well; especially rare, or specialist collectibles that are difficult to source offline (see Merrick Mint, PARTS TWO: DON'T RE-INVENT THE WHEEL!).

Although the young, largely male Internet audience does not tend to be interested in antiques, and the cost of postage can be prohibitive, collectables do tend to sell well. For example, stamps, coins and military memorabilia sell particularly well. Also, sports memorabilia is particularly in demand; everything from rare programs to replica shirts is considered collector's items. Sports souvenir programs are the most popular collectable but rare or old photographs are also valuable collector's items.

COMPUTER SUPPLIES

Being a computer-based industry, any related products have obvious appeal to the online audience. Most computer-literate, Internet-familiar consumers like to keep up with the latest computer technology.

PLATE 40: COMPUTER SUPPLIES WEBSITE

Therefore, as consumers consistently upgrade their computers there is a constant demand for the latest hardware and software products. Any online company that specializes in a specific sector of the home PC, business or computer games markets should see a demand for its goods.

COMPUTER MANUFACTURE

Building a computer is easier than it has ever been. It is relatively straightforward to get hold of the components, and because you are making it yourself it works out quite economical. It is no surprise then that many people are now building and selling PCs for a living, undercutting major manufacturers who have to meet much higher overheads and transport costs. Competitive advantage is often gained through offering a bespoke online service offering machines built to the specific specifications of the buyer (see SELLING HIGHLY CUSTOMIZED PRODUCTS). Niche market computers (i.e. highly specialized, specific-purpose computers) requiring highly-specialized hardware or extremely high specifications is a profitable business for a number of specialist computer assembly companies.

CONTENT PROVISION

'Content is King' and everyone that owns a website knows it! As the Internet becomes more and more popular and every new website needs to compete with ever-increasing numbers of direct competitors, the need for fresh content is becoming more important.

The main reason why people use the Internet is for information or entertainment. Therefore, the demand for new or unique content will continue to rise as companies strive to inform and entertain their customers. A stable income can be earned from providing news, information or entertainment such as quizzes, articles, cartoons, puzzles, 'a-to-z's and interactive games.

CONTEST HOSTING

Competitions attract visitors to websites. By setting up a website competition, third party companies, who may or may not have a web presence, may buy the e-mail addresses of those visitors to the website hosting the competition. Companies host contests, competitions and surveys to attract customers. To enter a competition the user must give their personal details. A database of everybody who enters the website should be kept, which is not difficult to set up, and the list can then be used to make further offers or sold to other companies.

CONTRACT FORMS

Template or fill-in-the-blank legal contracts are very popular and can serve a wide variety of uses, from a residential lease contract to home purchases to freelance contracts. Template contract forms can be sold to specialty office product retailers on a wholesale basis or directly to the public by creating a website that enables visitors to download contract templates for a fee. It will take time and careful research to develop the contract forms, but with that said the saleable lifespan for the product can be many years.

DATING WEBSITES

Advancements in matchmaking software has allowed for a host of options for providing a matchmaking service. With software now so cheap it might well be a good time to take advantage of this trend and start a Dating Service small business (see Positives Dating, PARTS TWO: DON'T RE-INVENT THE WHEEL!).

To help differentiate your business, you could offer personalized dating counseling services. You'll have to advertise aggressively in order to build your singles database and offer membership discounts in exchange for referrals. Your most important goal is building and maintaining your membership database.

Offer themed singles or consider partnering with other matchmaking services to build or quickly expand your membership base. Build a matchmaking website your members can use to share videos, photos, relationship preferences, personality profiles or chat with other members.

DIET AND FITNESS

As *Maslow's Hierarchy of Needs* tells us, any product or service that promises to improve people's looks or health is often good business. Therefore, one out of three women and one out of four men are on a diet at any given time.

A recent government survey indicated that 50 percent of American adults wanted to lose weight and start a regular diet and fitness program. And given the fact that there are more than 200 million adults in the U.S., this means there are potentially 100 million customers for any business venture that specializes in diet and fitness products and services.

PLATE 41: DIABETES DIET WEBSITE

Opportunities for a website dedicated to providing visitors with diet and fitness information and services are unlimited. Your website could provide users with diet and fitness information, products for sale, online fitness training and diet coaching and offer online fitness evaluations, or a combination of any or all of these products and services targeted at a specific market sector e.g. diabetics or pregnant women.

DIGITAL PHOTO STORAGE

Our precious old photographs are quickly being replaced by their digital counterparts. However, digital photographs do pose challenges. First, finding a particular photograph on your computer can take hours. Second, most consumers don't take the necessary precautions to protect their photos and risk losing all of them. An online digital photo storage resource is easy to set up, requiring only a website and large server space, and could be profitable if you specialize in storing a specific niche of images, such as pet photos, baby photos etc.

To help promote the website service you could write a series of articles or start a blog that provides tips and tricks for organizing digital photographs, how to take high quality photos, or digital camera reviews etc.

DIRECTORIES

Directories are in increasing demand because they help people focus the search for information. For example, every year students vie for educational scholarships, and one of the most difficult challenges facing them is trying to keep track and up-to-date with the thousands of different scholarships that are offered each year. Developing a website that features information about scholarships can serve two purposes.

PLATE 42: SCHOLARSHIP WEBSITE

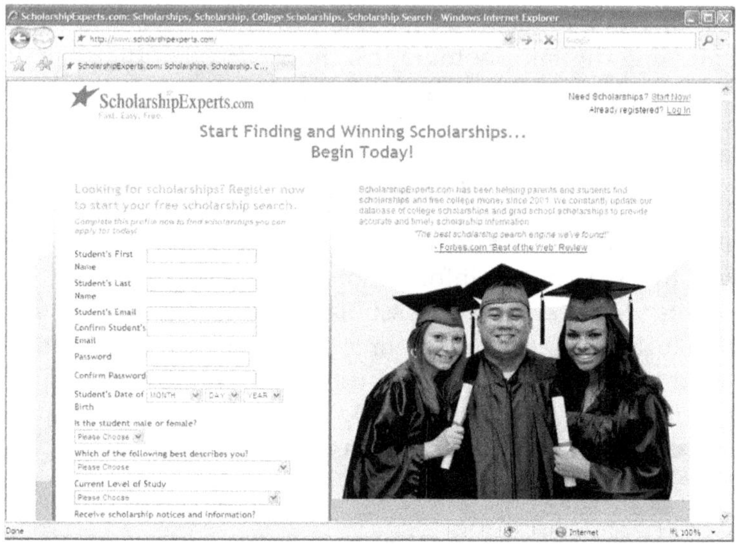

The first is that creating this type of website is a terrific way to develop your own home-based business. The second purpose is for parents and students to have access to a resource base to learn more about particular scholarships and the required criteria in terms of the awarding process.

This type of online business could earn revenue in a few ways, such as charging students and parents a yearly membership fee for access to the website or charging educational facilities and scholarship advisory boards a fee to post their scholarship information. Of course, advertising revenues could also be earned by renting banner ads once the website is established. This business option has a perfect *Strategic Fit*™ for the Internet.

E-BARGAINS

Simply put, you compile an e-mail address list of people that would like to receive your weekly e-bargains newsletter that features discounts on a wide variety of consumer products and services. There are no membership fees or costs associated with receiving the newsletter. Income is earned by selling a limited number of advertising spaces to online merchants and service providers that want exposure to your newsletter subscribers.

In addition to paying the advertising fee, you can have merchants and service providers provide the advertised products and service at a discount. You can also spice up your newsletter by including trivia questions, games, jokes or any other interesting content.

Be sure to comply with anti-spam regulations and remove anyone from your e-mail list that requests to opt out. Securing just five advertisers per week each paying $50 will create a yearly income in excess of $10,000 and, best of all; this can be accomplished with a part-time effort of less than 10 hours of work each week.

ENTERTAINMENT COUPONS

This business concept is very straightforward. Design a website that is indexed into various entertainment services and products such as musical concerts, plays, movies, etc, and then secure companies and businesses within the entertainment industry to advertise discounts that apply to their specific products and services on the website.

PLATE 43: COUPON WEBSITE

Visitors to the entertainment coupon website should be able to print discount coupons for the event or product they were seeking. The business would gain revenue by charging the entertainment companies a monthly fee to advertise on the website and post their discount coupons.

E-ZINE PUBLISHER

If you have an expertise or a passion for a specific hobby, activity, or general area of interest, you might consider starting an e-zine or newsletter publishing business. Your newsletter can contain articles, guides, 'how to's', event calendars, editorial opinions etc. You can earn revenue through subscriptions and advertising sales.

PLATE 44: AFFILIATE WEBSITE

Your content needs to be of interest or value to enough customers to motivate them to subscribe. Constantly solicit feedback from your members to continuously improve layout, features, and content. Also, you can generate revenue as follows:

- **Sell Advertisement Space** - businesses need to advertise and if you've got an e-zine that fits their target market, then you could sell them advertisement space. You could offer classified ads, solo ads, top spot ads, etc. The more targeted your subject and e-zine, the more you can charge for advertising.

- **Sell Your Own Products** – rather than using a shop front, you can target your subscribers with e-mail campaigns for specific, targeted offers of interest to your niche client base. A $19.95 digital product sold to 10% of 5,000 subscribers will make you almost $10,000 per campaign.

- **Monthly Membership** - you could publish your e-zine at least 5 times per month. And if you charged $19.95 per subscriber, and you get 500 or more people each paying you every month, this can add up to nearly $10,000 per month.

FRANCHISE AND LICENSING OPPORTUNITIES

As a Franchise and Licensing Consultant you'll help potential franchise investors understand the franchise process, laws and regulations, financial requirements, and ongoing commitments. Therefore, a solid understanding of franchises is needed.

Create a website that brings corporations with franchise opportunities for sale together with people that want to purchase and operate a franchise business. The website can be created in a directory format with a main index page that lists the various franchise opportunity categories on the website, such as restaurants and food services, retail and maintenance services. You may also want to develop a franchise newsletter to keep your customers informed about franchise trends and developments.

Income is earned by charging corporations a listing fee to be featured on the website. Additionally, an alliance could be established with a lawyer that specializes in franchise agreements to write and post articles pertaining to the legalities of franchising on the website. Promote the website by using Internet marketing techniques such as SEO, links and joining a rotating banner advertisement program.

GENEALOGICAL RESEARCHER

This particular niche takes the B2B research model and brings it to the B2C sector. Almost everybody likes to know their roots and it is a growing interest, with thousands of people joining genealogical societies in countries across the globe. As a genealogical researcher, you'll research into family histories and construct family trees.

You'll need experience in genealogical research, and an organized, detail-oriented personality. You'll need a computer with an inkjet or laser printer, the usual office software, genealogy software and Internet access. The advantage to this business is that you can start with a minimum investment.

Your clients will be people who want to discover their family histories. You can attract their business by writing articles and targeting advertising at special-interest groups like Civil War re-enactors and historical societies.

GRAPHIC ART

Art, clip art, graphics, animation and cartoons are in great demand as website managers seek to include added-value entertainment content to their websites. Due to the web being a graphics-orientated medium, any design-based industry should be able to use its website to advertise and sell its design skills. For example, some design companies allow customers to design their own business cards online. Other companies offer a full graphic design service from their website.

HERBAL GOODS

Organic, holistic living is becoming more and more popular every day, especially with the current Internet audience. Consumers continue to look for products that are not only natural but also may provide homeopathic benefits. As many of your customers will be new to herbal products you can educate them on the various types and benefits of the products you sell.

PLATE 45: HERBAL PRODUCTS WEBSITE

In addition to selling herbs and related products, your business can also provide consulting services to help educate customers on the use and benefit of each product line you sell.

It is worth noting that to protect yourself and your clients, you should purchase your herbal products from only reputable, qualified wholesalers. To help build a client base, keep your business fresh in your customers' minds by distributing a small herbal products e-newsletter or e-magazine.

MUSIC SALES

Similar to books, music is well suited to the virtual market space. However, with so much music of all types readily available, it would seem difficult to find an untapped niche that is both sizable and profitable but has not already been exploited.

PLATE 46: MUSIC WEBSITE

However, if you can find an under-serviced, profitable niche in this sector then you are almost guaranteed to make money. Rather than concentrating on selling niche genres of music (e.g. selling just Rap, Country and Western, Rock etc.), perhaps you could concentrate on providing music that is suitable to a niche market (e.g. music appropriate to fashion shops, nurseries, boutique hotels, health spas etc.).

PRESCRIPTION DRUGS AND VITAMINS

Due to the exceptionally high cost of prescription drugs in the US, there is a large and growing demand for online sales of all kinds of medication, including vitamins and health supplements.

In addition to selling drugs and vitamins, you can also include articles and information about the health benefits of medication and vitamin supplements as well as an online chat room so visitors can exchange information.

To keep startup investment to a minimum, you can arrange a drop-ship agreement with one or more of the hundreds of companies that produce the drugs and vitamins. Basically, you sell the goods via your website, forward the orders electronically to the producer, and they fulfill the order and ship the product directly to your customers.

Note: anti-aging drugs are becoming a huge market online. This business model has the perfect *Strategic Fit*™ for the Internet.

REFERRALS

People are busy and don't have the time to look through the Yellow Pages and call around for quotes and credentials when trying to find an attorney, child care, or someone to fix their toilet. Therefore, creating a network of suppliers, checking their credentials, charging them a referral fee, and starting a company to provide referrals to busy clientele is an excellent way to earn online income.

A referral service or agency is basically a service with a toll free number that people call to obtain information on the product or service you are referring. Such websites refer daycares, doctors, realtors, restaurants, dentists, loan companies, photographers, etc.

You can refer almost anything you want; however, you'll need to maintain a list of quality providers for those that use your service. One of the most famous referral services is 1-800-DENTIST, a toll-free service where users can call and find recommended dentists in their area.

PLATE 47: REFERRAL WEBSITE

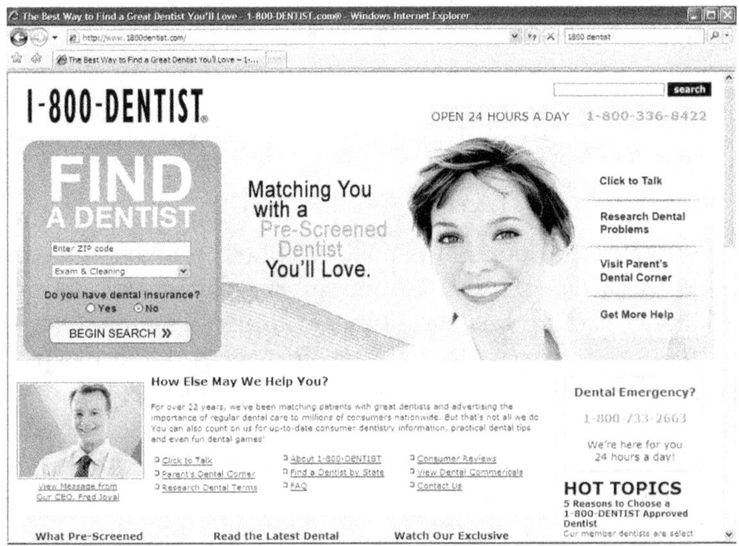

Operating a referral business requires you to provide a service for two separate parties; the contractor and the end user. You'll earn a commission for each referral from the contractor.

SELLING HIGHLY CUSTOMIZED PRODUCTS

In some cases all products manufactured by a small business can be highly customized. A product with a lot of customizable options may be difficult to sell via traditional channels. However, if your product is highly customized or is a highly specialized item, and if the product is targeted to a very narrow audience, this may be commercially successful online due to the huge potential market the Internet provides. If your product appeals to the Net audience it should sell well on the Internet.

The Internet is also a good advertising tool for purchases that are handled with "absolute confidentiality and discretion" and for which the company guarantees "complete and total privacy". Shoppers may often appreciate an anonymous ordering system for embarrassing purchases. "Made-to-measure" items and "one-offs" are also likely to sell well as customers often surf the Net in hope of finding products that are unique, authentic or not readily available locally.

SELLING OTHER PEOPLE'S PRODUCTS

(AFFILIATE SALES)

If you want to start an online business but don't have the space to keep a large amount of inventory, you could start an Affiliate Marketing business. Certain reputable companies on the Internet will pay to have their banner advertisements displayed on your company's website. Others will pay commission to you for selling their products.

To collect your sales commission you usually have to amass a sufficient or fixed amount of sales before a check is sent to you (e.g. $100). The procedure for operating an affiliate program is simple and costs nothing. Once the online registration form, and all codes, instructions etc. have been filled out, all relevant information will be forwarded.

As an affiliate marketer, your business will showcase other company's (your "affiliate partner's") products and services on your website. When a visitor to your website buys your partner's products, you get a percentage of the online sales.

While being an affiliate can be a very good home-based business opportunity, it will take time to build your website and attract sufficient visitors. As always, it is essential to build a high quality website and add unique and related subject content in addition to your affiliate products.

As you gain experience with your affiliate marketing business you can expand to include drop shipping products as well. The drop shipping model allows you to sell products directly from your website but, rather than your business shipping the product, you'll tell a wholesaler where to ship the goods.

SELLING TICKETS

Ticket sales of all kinds have proven to be a business well suited to e-commerce, even for bookings requiring significant amounts, such as air tickets.

PLATE 48: TICKET RETAILER WEBSITE

This is an example of how the public are prepared to browse the web if it results in cheaper prices, especially if the Internet gives customers access to the same data as any "middle man" or agent.

SEX SITES

The undeniable reality of Internet commerce is that it is dominated by sex; 70 to 80 per cent of every hit is a search for pornographic material. It should not be surprising that with a huge audience of young, single males, most Internet enquiries are sex-related. Gay or straight sex is one thing that this demographic sector is guaranteed to have an interest in. Censorship on the Net is minimal so the explicitness and diversity of sex-related websites on the web matches the appetite for it. At present there is an insatiable appetite for Net pornography.

Finding a niche in the sex industry is not difficult; there is a guaranteed audience for every sexual interest imaginable.

Once you have chosen your target niche, it is essential to attract, maintain and expand your customer base by using every facility available to you, including regularly updated content, member interaction and social networking facilities. The proven money-making model for this type of online business is revenue from a monthly membership subscription.

SHAREWARE

The general idea behind shareware is that software is offered free of charge for people to try before they commit themselves to a purchase. Customers are only asked to pay for it if they continue to find the product useful after a certain length of time.

PLATE 49: SHAREWARE WEBSITE

Normally, shareware is software, often a scaled-down version of a full product, but it does not have to be. Reports, information, or any other kind of service, can be offered on a "shareware" basis. If you have a digital product that can be offered as shareware, then it can work as a very effective way of introducing your product to the market.

SHAREWARE HOSTING

Another option is to become a shareware website for other vendors by agreeing to devote a small part of your website to the promotion of their wares, in exchange for a percentage of any licensing fees sold. Becoming a recognized source of shareware may also work well in improving your hit rates.

SOFTWARE ENGINEERING

Many computer programmers with skills in high-demand languages, such as Visual Basic, Java, C++ etc., now work freelance from home. Most promote their specialist programs through shareware and sell the code over the Internet.

With so many sectors of the business community now taking up computer-based commercial systems, there is an increasing demand for various computer programs. A freelance software engineer who can produce specialized programs for niche market businesses can achieve extremely profitable global sales.

SOUVENIRS SALES

Souvenirs, similar to collectibles, tend to sell well online. Securing a profitable niche of a specific market sector should be your aim.

PLATE 50: SOUVENIR WEBSITE

Note: If your company develops an attractive or trendy brand for its website it may be able to sell "quality merchandise" on the back of it. You may add your company's logo to T-shirts, mouse mats, mugs, pens and more. Many companies make more money from merchandising than from their original products or services.

SURVEYS

There are two ways of making cash from surveys or market research reports:

1. Your company can charge a fee to a client company for including their survey on your website.

2. You can conduct your own survey and then sell the results to other companies that are interested in your website visitors.

From the smallest independent businesses to the largest international corporations, businesses often rely on public opinion surveys to learn more about their products, services, competition, and customers. Public opinion polls and surveys can be conducted on the telephone, by mail, e-mail, website polling or personal interview.

TRAVEL

In only a few years the online travel industry has already become a crowded market. Airline tickets, online booking services, online car hire reservations, package holidays, tourist information, hotel and restaurant reviews, menus, prices and weather forecasting are all services offered on the web.

The very competitive nature of the travel industry means that consumers are now used to "shopping around" for deals on holidays and flights; hence the popularity of companies such as LastMinute.com (www.lastminute.com). However, only the larger companies can realistically offer cheap deals. Therefore, as the market nears saturation, any small business entering this sector should focus on specialization and developing niche markets and perhaps targeting only affluent and Internet-familiar countries such as America, Japan and Germany.

Small companies that specialize in themed and promotional events have witnessed an increased demand from all over the world since advertising online.

Many of the above opportunities can be used in combination within a company's commercial website to add value to its own website and hopefully create a profitable ongoing revenue stream.

In order to succeed against the travel industry's large brands and the do-it-yourselfers, you need to appeal to a specific group, or meet a need that has so far been unmet. For example, senior citizens may enjoy traveling, but may not be comfortable using the Internet to compare packages and prices. Perhaps you can develop vacation packages that would provide adventure and companionship for older adults.

Sports aficionados might love a theme-based vacation, following their favorite football or basketball team on the road.

Maybe you could base your business on developing the perfect family vacation packages. Or maybe you would like to specialize in honeymoons in unusual, romantic locations. Once you have determined your niche you can target that market.

You'll Make $ERIOUS
MONEY Online!

PART THREE

THE GOLDEN SECRETS
OF BUSINESS SUCCESS

Chapter Eight

The Reasons Why Online Businesses Fail

WHY DO ONLINE BUSINESSES FAIL?

It's a fact; the majority of new businesses fail within the first few years, and only a tiny percentage remain in business after ten years. But Why?

Well, one of the main reasons for this low success rate is sheer exhaustion – the owners wear themselves out keeping a flawed business model ticking over through over-working. This is a lesson I've learnt to my cost – hard work hides a bad business model!

That's why it is so important to get the business model right as early as possible in the business development cycle; ideally, before launch. If the business concept is a really good one then it won't require excessive man hours or physical work.

> "No institution can possibly survive if it needs geniuses or supermen to manage it. It must be organized in such a way as to be able to get along under a leadership composed of average human beings."
>
> Peter Drucker

Not that hard work should be an issue, but the worst possible reason for starting a new business is for a better "work-life balance". If you're looking for a quieter life, don't start your own business!

> "I do not believe a man can ever leave his business.
> He ought to think of it by day and dream of it by night."
> Henry Ford

That's why a passion for what you do is so important (as well as a profitable niche and demand for what you sell).

In this part of the book I cover 'best practice'; what to do and what not to do. I'll use 'The 10 Reasons Why Online Businesses Fail' as a guide to help you avoid common mistakes and help your business succeed. If you follow the advice and concepts covered here you'll stand a significantly better chance of making, and keeping, serious money online.

THE TOP 10 REASONS WHY ONLINE BUSINESSES FAIL

1. A Poorly Designed Business Model
2. Poor Management
3. Insufficient Capital
4. Over-Extension
5. Failure to Identify and Exploit a Niche
6. Failure to Create a Unique Proposition Strategy
7. Failure to Build Long-Term Value
8. Poor Marketing
9. Poor Product Strategy
10. Failure to Establish an Effective Team

You'll Make $ERIOUS
MONEY Online!

Chapter Nine

A Profitable Business Model

REASON FOR FAILURE #1
A POORLY DESIGNED BUSINESS MODEL

This refers to the fact that if your business has the wrong *Strategic Fit*™ for e-commerce then it will inevitably struggle. Lack of planning, such as not using the *Risk Eliminator*™ system or *Strategic Fit Matrix*™, will inevitably lead to failure.

> "By failing to prepare, you are preparing to fail."
> Benjamin Franklin

It is critical for all businesses to develop a workable and efficient business model; this should be outlined in a detailed business plan. Many small businesses fail because of fundamental shortcomings in their business planning. Any plan must be realistic and based on accurate, current information and educated projections for the future.

Part of designing a business model is to conduct the due diligence required to establish that there is a viable market for your product or service. Since approximately 90% of startups fail because they can't find a market for their product or service, it is vital that you use tools such as the *Risk Eliminator*™ system to help save you thousands of dollars in development costs and a great deal of heart ache.

MASTERING THE 5 INGREDIENTS OF ANY SUCCESSFUL BUSINESS

Have you mastered these five parts of your business?

1. Product/Service
2. Legalities
3. Systems
4. Communication
5. Cash Flow

PRODUCT/SERVICE

Most businesses sell a product or service of some kind, even if these are defined as 'information' products or services. To be successful you'll have to acquire an in-depth knowledge about the product or service you sell. If you don't have in-depth knowledge of what you sell you'll lose credibility and respect in the eyes of your team, which can contribute to you losing control of your business – ultimately causing you to lose your customers.

> "There is no substitute for accurate knowledge. Know yourself, know your business, know your men."
> Lee Iacocca

LEGALITIES

In terms of how much you could stand to lose, similar to health and safety regulations, knowledge of the legal side of commerce is vital. Knowledge of company incorporation (legal entity), tax, IP protection (patent, trademark, copyright etc.), licensing, permits, contracts etc. is a vital part of being a good business person. Learn as much as you can.

> "Obedience of the law is demanded; not asked as a favor."
> Theodore Roosevelt

SYSTEMS

Similar to product or service knowledge, your knowledge of the systems involved in the manufacturing, ordering, inventory, sales fulfillment, software, customer services, accounting, invoicing, payments and telecommunications in your business is important because, unless you have an understanding of them, how they are used may be taken out of your control. You'll also be less informed when making financial and strategic decisions that can affect the direction of your business. Regardless of the systems you adopt, always be aware of the data they produce.

> "Data is a precious thing and will last longer than the systems themselves."
>
> Tim Berners-Lee

COMMUNICATION

'Communication' includes the advertising, marketing, sales, public relations, word-of-mouth, good reputation, good relationships, good will, product/service explanation and promotion, and brand recognition, as well as the partnerships and strategic alliances your business uses. Ultimately, how you communicate to people determines how they think about your business, and what they think about it inevitably determines how successful your business will be. Practice your communication skills.

> "The way we communicate with others and with ourselves ultimately determines the quality of our lives."
>
> Tony Robbins

CASH FLOW

'Cash is King'. In-depth knowledge of your company's cash cycle (i.e. money in, money out, instant payments, pre-payments, direct debits, 30, 60, 90 or 120 day invoicing, debt factoring, payroll, insurances, rent, bills etc.) is probably the most important knowledge of all. Cash flow is the blood that keeps flowing through it, keeping it alive. Without it your business is dead, so keep checking its pulse!

> "Happiness is a positive cash flow."
> Fred Adler

YOUR ORGANIZATION'S STRUCTURE, CULTURE AND ETHOS

Every company has its own unique culture and way of doing things. Ideally, your business should be built around the following three elements:

1. A Mission
2. Leadership
3. Teamwork

It will help your cause if you have a collective 'mission'. A mission can be an attitude, a process, and a target that every member of your organization follows with enthusiasm.

> "I rate enthusiasm even above professional skill."
> Edward Appleton

To help your employees follow your mission they will have to have to be led. Good leadership is a combination of good motivation, management and organizational skills as well as communicational skills to help get the message behind your mission across.

> "Communication is about being effective, not always about being proper."
> Bo Bennett

Teamwork is essential; you'll need a collective work ethic to achieve the mission. Try to develop a team of specialists and experts with as much talent as you can afford.

124

"First, make yourself a reputation for being a creative
genius. Second, surround yourself with partners who are
better than you are. Third, leave them to go get on with it."
David Ogilvy

Always try to employ people smarter than you and don't be
afraid of sharing trade secrets with them; the fact is that 99% of
people prefer a safe wage rather than take the boss's ideas and
starting their own business (though it never hurts to separate
people or departments so no one person knows everything!).

"It's not what you pay a man, but what he costs you
that counts."
Will Rogers

When hiring help, always remember, 'hire slowly, fire
quickly!' Take your time to find the right person and if they're
not working out then replace them as fast as possible before
they become a bad influence on your business' staff and
culture.

"Success or failure in business is caused more by the
mental attitude even than by mental capacities."
Walter Scott

Also, always hire on attitude before talent or qualifications.
If they've got the right attitude they can learn the work, be an
asset, and not cost you money or cause trouble.

"Attitude is more important than the past, than education,
than money, than circumstances, than what people do or say.
It is more important than appearance, giftedness, or skill."
W. C. Fields

Although you ultimately will probably want to develop a
business model that functions without your input, initially it is
usually the case that a new business owner needs to contribute
at least one (if not all) of the functions and processes of a
business.

Try to develop an overall knowledge of all your business' processes and functions but try to outsource or employ in-house for at least two of the three functions as soon as possible. This will allow you to use your expertise in one of the more vital functions.

Reaching the point where you only have to contribute one part of the business' process is a significant milestone. It will allow you to concentrate on what you do best, allowing the business to be more efficient and productive.

There are basically three processes to most businesses:

1. Work In
2. Work Done
3. Work Out

'Work In' refers to the process of attracting work. This might be through advertising, sales or marketing. 'Work Done' is the actual making or acquiring of the product, service or information the business actually sells. 'Work Out' means the fulfillment, logistics and distribution of the business' product, service or information.

Most of your company's success and growth will probably occur when you can step back entirely from the daily fire-fighting of processes and administration and concentrate on the bigger picture; strategy.

Strategy is closely tied in with the whole business process/cycle your company will follow. It's an advantage to know what the typical business process/cycle is so that you can base your company's strategy around it. No two businesses' development is identical but it helps to know what the road map to success looks like (see overleaf).

THE 10 STEPS OF THE BUSINESS PROCESS/CYCLE:

1. **Business Idea**
2. **Research** (setup costs, competitor analysis, defining a target market)
3. **Product/Service Development or Prototyping**
4. **Design Business Model** (premises, employees, hardware, software, skills, resources, processes, USP, UVP, packaging, distribution, payment processing, marketing, returns, customer service etc.)
5. **Business Plan** (especially financials – i.e. costs, debt facilities etc)
6. **Legalities:** Business' legal entity (i.e. legal liability), incorporation, tax, IP protection, licensing, permits, contracts etc.
7. **Putting the Resources Together** (e.g. build the team)
8. **Start:** Put the process in place.
9. **Build Barriers to Entry** (leverage all your competitive advantages to make it impractical for potential competitors to compete)
10. **Expand:** cut costs, build in synergies, leverage, train, improve, research, develop, invest etc.

You'll Make $ERIOUS
MONEY Online!

Chapter Ten

Effective Management

REASON FOR FAILURE #2
POOR MANAGEMENT

Poor management, such as failing to keep overhead costs low, failing to control the controllable costs, failing to prepare for volatility of uncontrollable costs, poor internal controls and execution, poor customer service, accounting controls, theft or fraud prevention etc. are all common contributing factors to a failing business.

> "One of the tests of leadership is the ability to recognize
> a problem before it becomes an emergency."
> Arnold H. Glasow

New business owners frequently lack the relevant business and management expertise in areas such as finance, purchasing, selling, production, or hiring and managing employees. Unless you recognize what you don't do well, and seek help, you may soon face disaster. Always be positive and ensure that everything is put in place to improve processes, not hinder them.

> "Most of what we call management consists of making
> it difficult for people to get their work done."
> Peter Drucker

Neglect of a business can also be its downfall. Take care to regularly study, organize, plan and control all activities of its operations. This includes the continuing study of market research and customer data, an area which may be more prone to disregard once a business has been established.

"Effective leadership is putting first things first.
Effective management is discipline, carrying it out."
Stephen Covey

If you employ people, strive to be a good leader who creates a work climate that encourages productivity and accountability.

"Great companies have high cultures of accountability...
and I think our culture is strong on that."
Steve Ballmer

You should be able to hire competent people, train them and be able to delegate. A good leader is also skilled at strategic thinking, able to make a vision a reality, and able to confront change, make transitions, and envision new possibilities for the future with enthusiasm.

"Enthusiasm is the yeast that makes your hopes shine to
the stars. Enthusiasm is the sparkle in your eyes, the swing
in your gait. The grip of your hand, the irresistible surge of
will and energy to execute your ideas."
Henry Ford

NOW, WHAT'S THE PLAN?

You must plan. First you need to have a vision for your business. What are your business goals? How are you going to achieve those goals? What are you going to sell? How are you going to find and service customers so you can grow? Answers to these questions should be written in your business plan. All banks or potential investors will request a business plan if you are seeking to secure addition capital for your company.

Second, you need to plan your time. If you are a disorganized mess, with 'to do' lists on scrap paper all over your desk, it's time to get a planner and use it. Your business needs your guidance, if you cannot manage your time, how will you manage your business?

"Time is the scarcest resource and unless it is managed nothing else can be managed."

Peter Drucker

If you lack current and relevant experience in finance, purchasing, selling, production, hiring and managing employees, get help!

When you reach a critical level (about 1 million to 5 million dollars of turnover), be sure to put a proper management structure in place that will make the work flow and information flow optimal, without your business losing its dynamism. Also, this is the time when you should hire suitable managers.

Always be open to new opportunities. Take advantage of anything with a government grant or support (e.g. education or health related). Keep an eye out for new technology or trends. For example, every new device seems to require a protective cover for it (usually in numerous bright colors). Also, every new technology leads to another complimentary product or service, and another possible business opportunity. The downside is often that these opportunities are often short lived.

3... 2... 1...

Try not to over-spend on things you don't really need, especially at launch. Keep your initial outlay to a minimum; you don't need the latest, most expensive equipment, just enough to do the job and be profitable. Only after you make a profit should you spend money on upgrading the infrastructure of your business process. Always ask yourself these questions:

1. Will this make more than it costs?
2. How long will this take to pay for itself?

Cash is King

"Turnover is vanity, Profit is sanity". It's the cash in the bank that matters, not turnover or estimated sales. Make sure you know your cash projections. You need to know who is going to pay you, why they are paying you and when they will be paying you.

Cash flows in and out of a business at different times and in different amounts. That's why you should always keep an eye on your cash, and always keep reserves. It is imperative that you know that you'll have the cash to pay salaries and unexpected bills.

Always overestimate your costs, and underestimate your income. Avoid making your business success dependent on attaining unrealistic profits in unrealistic timescales. The financial predictions outlined in your business plan will influence all your business decisions, including:

- Staff numbers
- Stock levels
- Size of premises
- Web hosting requirements
- Hardware requirements
- Telecommunications requirements

Therefore, never base your business predictions on guesswork; do everything you can to research actual or realistic costs, cash flow, turnover and profit levels.

"Assumption is the mother of all f**k up's!"
Travis Dane

GO WITH THE (CASH) FLOW

One of the major reasons why businesses fail is that they grow too big too quickly and soon their expenditures are larger than their income; they simply don't have the cash available to pay bills and salaries when required.

The advantage of a cash flow forecast is that you can predict when you'll require cash. Bills need to be paid at different times; for example, suppliers may need to be paid after 30, 60 or 90 days, and some customers may buy on credit. Also, as your business grows, you may borrow more and your expenditures may increase.

AVOID DEPENDENCE

Don't gamble all your money on one venture, one advertising campaign or one client. Prepare for certain things to fail and learn from them. Eventually you'll be able to adapt and improve things, but only if you have been able to survive the mistakes, mishaps and bad times. So make sure you are prepared mentally, commercially and financially.

If you depend on one customer, one product, one supplier, one form of advertising, one member of staff, one piece of equipment, one means of collecting money, one skill or one channel to market, then you are risking the immediate failure of your business if you should lose them.

The more you rely on a single point of failure, the more likely it is to fail. Therefore, ensure that you have backups, fallbacks and alternatives. Also, try to build a 'network' business structure (with several products, sales channels and clients) rather than a 'chain' business structure (with one single product, sales channel and client) so that if one element of the business structure fails then the rest of the business is not affected.

FIVE FORMULAS EVERY ONLINE BUSINESS NEEDS TO KNOW

Here are five formulas that will help you analyze your business.

TRAFFIC ANALYSIS

Once you have traffic coming to your website, you'll want to learn about conversion rates and tweak your landing page to improve your conversion rate as much as possible.

CONVERSION RATE ANALYSIS

To help your company become profitable and control costs it is imperative that you know statistics such as how many visitors you are converting into customers and how much each customer is costing you. Below are a few conversion formulas every successful online business keeps an eye on.

1. How many visitors are you converting into customers?
Your *Visitor-to-Customer Conversion Rate* is one of the easiest stats to gather, but also one of the most powerful. It's a quick indication of how effectively you're convincing visitors to buy from you.

$$\text{(\# of sales / \# of visitors)} \times 100 = \text{Visitor-to-Customer Conversion Rate}$$

So if you get 10,000 visitors a month and 472 of them become customers, then your conversion rate is 4.7%.

$$(472 / 10,000) \times 100 = 4.7\%$$

2. How many visitors are signing up for your newsletter?
Known as the *Visitor-to-Subscriber Conversion Rate*, this metric tells you how attractive your subscription offer is. Keep an eye on this figure as you test different positions and copy for your sign-up form.

$$\text{(\# of subscribers / \# of visitors)} \times 100 = \text{Visitor-to-Subscriber Conversion Rate}$$

If you get 10,000 new visitors to your website in a week and 2,730 of them subscribe to your free newsletter, then your conversion rate is 27%.

$$(\ 2{,}730\ /10{,}000) \times 100 = 27\%$$

3. How many of your newsletter subscribers are becoming customers?
Your *Subscriber-to-Customer Conversion Rate* is a good test of how effective a sales tool your newsletter is. This is especially important if your main product is a paid newsletter.

$$\text{(\# of customers / \# of subscribers)} \times 100 = \text{Subscriber-to-Customer Conversion Rate}$$

If 120 of your 2,730 subscribers end up buying something from you, then your subscriber-to-customer conversion rate is 4.4%.

$$(120\ /2{,}730) \times 100 = 4.4\%$$

4. How much revenue are you making from each visitor?
This *Revenue per Visitor* statistic shows how much you're earning from your average visitor. This is particularly valuable since this number helps determine how much you can spend to acquire a new visitor while still earning a profit.

$$\text{sales / \# of visitors} = \text{Revenue per Visitor}$$

If you sold $6,000 worth of inventory this month and had 39,000 visitors to your website, you would know your revenue per visitor is $0.15.

$$\$6,000 / 39,000 = \$0.15$$

5. How many people are clicking where you want them to click?
Your Click-through Rate shows the percentage of people who "click through" from your sales letter to your order form (or any other link you want to measure).

(clicks on link x /# of visitors to page with link x) x 100 = Click-through Rate

For example, if you get 10,000 visitors to your sales letter, and 650 click on the link to your order form, then your sales letter has a click-through rate of 6.5%.

(650 0,000) x 100 = 6.5%

Chapter Eleven

Ensuring Sufficient Capital

REASON FOR FAILURE #3
INSUFFICIENT CAPITAL

Poor capital structure, reliance on critical financing that dries up, or over-capitalization are the most common reasons why a company runs out of capital. For example, companies very often take on too much debt or lack sufficient cash flow.

> "Rule No.1: Never lose money. Rule No.2: Never forget rule No.1."
>
> Warren Buffett

A common fatal mistake for many failed businesses is having insufficient operating funds. Business owners underestimate how much money is needed and they are forced to close before they even have had a fair chance to succeed. They also may have an unrealistic expectation of incoming revenues from sales.

It is imperative to ascertain how much money your business will require; not only the costs of *starting*, but the costs of *staying* in business. It is important to take into consideration that many businesses take a year or two to become profitable. This means you'll need enough funds to cover all costs until sales can eventually pay for these costs; you may also require outside funding to meet all costs.

RAISING CAPITAL

To achieve rapid and sustained growth, sooner or later you may have to attract financiers to raise capital. Raising capital through private investors is one of the best ways to get a new company off the ground.

Private individuals, such as angel investors or venture capitalists, whom contribute their skills as well as their money to help new companies, are the best options for raising capital. They can provide your business with extra working capital that can be used for marketing, purchasing property, purchasing another business, or for just about anything else to assist the growth of your business. Any investor will want to make at least 30 percent on their investment, so if you can guarantee *that* you'll almost always find a willing investor for your business.

Once you find investors you need to make sure you have a good funding proposal in place. The investors will want to see in-depth information on how much money you need to run your business, and they also want to see how that money will be spent. You also need to have an 'exit' strategy planned out for the investors; showing how money will be earned and paid back.

When developing a capital-acquisition strategy, ask yourself the following questions:

1. How much do you need?
2. When do you need it?
3. From whom do you want it?
4. What kind of investment do you need?
5. What compromises will you accept?

1. How much do you need?

Take more than you think you need (but only if it's cheap). Cash can be cheap, but equity never is; recovering any percentage of your company is very difficult and very expensive. In the start-up phase, when your company's value is low, multiple, small financing rounds are often a more cost-effective way of acquiring money.

Calculate how much money you require, given specific milestones (e.g. company launch, expanding your sales force or equipment etc.). Then, add that figure to your total operational costs. Ideally, you should also add a safety-net of six to nine months of operational costs to that figure. The aim is to raise sufficient capital to (i) keep the company running, and (ii) achieve specific milestones. Achieving these goals will demonstrate increased value before your next round of fundraising. Therefore, try to schedule your financing rounds so that you can demonstrate success, that way you'll acquire higher valuations and keep your investors and stakeholders happy.

2. When do you need it?

Raise money before you need it (you always need it sooner than you think). The financing process always takes longer than anticipated. For example, bank loans can take more than three months, while grants and venture capital can take up to 12 months to come through. Inevitably, you'll have to be able to produce evidence of hitting pre-defined milestones.

3. From whom do you want it?

Only accept money from a person or organization you like, respect and trust, and that understands the industry sector your company is in. Investors may only be with you for the short to medium term (several years) but you'll go through tough times together.

4. What kind of investment do you need?

There are basically two kinds of investment; 'active' and 'passive' investment.
   1. Active money is from financiers who will work with you closely (usually knowledgeable of your industry, they'll add value by introducing you to sales prospects, influential people etc.
   2. Passive money is just money (no connections, no additional value).

Note: If your company is a new one, or if the financier brings added-value, you should take active money. If you just need cash, take passive money.

5. What compromises will you accept?

Don't be greedy (but don't get ripped off!). If you require equity financing, you'll need to sell shares of your company, repeatedly. But as the cake gets bigger, the increasing number of slices gets smaller; this is called 'dilution'. For example, if you start out by owning 100% of a company, pre-financing, don't be surprised if you own 20% or less at the exit. This is because initially you'll sell off big slices (often 20% to 40%) at each financing round.

Giving up *equity* is one compromise, but loss of *control* is another. Investors should make up only 20% to 40% of the company's board. It's worth taking a lower valuation to get a stronger group of investors; strong, active investors can make all the difference—not only in building the company but in future financing rounds and helping raise cash when it is really required.

Note: The higher your company's valuation, the higher the financing terms. A company's valuation is based on perception; if you present your company with passion (showcasing all the good positives) you may well receive considerable financial backing.

MANAGING LATE PAYMENTS

FACT: The major reason why businesses have to close down is bankruptcy.

Even if things don't get that drastic, small business owners wind up with unpaid financial obligations they wonder how they're going to repay. The number one cause of this problem is late payment – ruining the company's cash flow.

Cash flow is the blood flow that keeps a business alive. Without sufficient capital, a company cannot make its product or provide its service. If it can't make its product or provide its service, it can't sell its product or service. If it can't sell its product or service, it can't make any money.

Unfortunately, as heavy debt forces businesses to be selective about bill payments (paying some bills one month while others are held over to the next), often, the small business owner compensates the lack of funds by using their personal bank account to pay the additional (and often unanticipated) expenses of their business.

When that money runs out, the business owner starts to wonder how long it's going to be before the companies that he or she purchased from start demanding their money. That is why, as soon as it is financially feasible, it is vital for any business to acquire the following accounting facilities:

1. Take payments in advance (whenever possible)
2. Keep accurate automated records of customer payments
3. Develop recurring revenue streams

Note: Due to facilities such as credit card processing and accounting software, e-commerce provides the best possible environment for all these facilities.

MANAGING OVERHEADS

Obviously, not all financial problems are due to consumers' late payment; managing hundreds of customer accounts, payment plans, credit card transactions, budgeting, tax records, creating invoices, income and expense accounts can become overwhelming. Keeping up to date with your accounts can be even more overwhelming when it results in you missing the opportunities to actually make more money.

Here are three financial rules that small businesses should follow:

> 1. Payment expectations should be consistent and clear to customers
> 2. Have a "No Payment, No Product" Policy (whenever possible)
> 3. Have an automated payment collection process

Note: Again, online software and facilities makes these rules viable.

REAPING THE REWARDS OF RECURRING REVENUE

The secret to ending your cash flow worries is recurring revenue. The best form of recurring revenue is 'passive' (no physical work required) revenue from digital products, such as software, e-books or information, that can be downloaded or emailed automatically.

If you want to create lifelong customers you should consider developing recurring revenue streams over extended periods of time, such as a monthly 'product'. For example, try to create a monthly subscription, a "members-only" blog or forum, value-embedded DVDs, monthly membership, an executive members club, or any revenue sources whereby you can "sign 'em up" for life.

Once you have the trust of your regular customers, they are extremely likely to want to become one of your exclusive customers. Because they know you'll deliver, they'll be glad to pay for future products or services.

Chapter Twelve

Avoiding Over-Extension

REASON FOR FAILURE #4
OVER-EXTENSION

Over-expansion (and over-capitalization) often occurs when business owners confuse success with how fast they can expand their business. A focus on slow and steady growth is optimum. Many a bankruptcy has been caused by rapidly expanding companies that spend their initial cash before it is flowing in at a positive rate. To avoid this situation, the first financial data you need to know is the number you need to achieve to break-even.

BREAK-EVEN POINT CALCULATION

The break-even point (BEP) for a product is the point where total revenue received equals the total costs associated with the sale of the product (TR=TC).

Break even analysis can be used to analyze the potential profitability of an expenditure in a sales-based business. A break-even point is also typically calculated in order for businesses to determine if it would be profitable to sell a proposed product, as opposed to attempting to modify an existing product, so it can be made profitable.

Break Even Point (sales) = fixed cost/contribution (pu) * sp (pu)

Break Even Point (output) = fixed cost/contribution per unit

Contribution (p.u) = selling price (p.u) - variable cost (p.u)

BENEFITS OF BREAK-EVEN ANALYSIS

The main advantage of break-even analysis is that it explains the relationship between costs, production volume and returns. Break-even analysis is most useful when used with partial budgeting or capital budgeting techniques. The major benefit to using break-even analysis is that it indicates the lowest amount of business activity necessary to prevent losses.

Calculation of the BEP can be made using the following formula:

$$BEP = TFC / (SUP\text{-}VCUP)$$

BER = break-even point (units of production)
TFC = total fixed costs
SUP = selling price per unit of production
VCUP = variable costs per unit of production

LIMITATIONS OF BREAK-EVEN ANALYSIS

- It is best suited to the analysis of one product at a time;
- it may be difficult to classify a cost as all variable or all fixed; and
- there may be a tendency to continue to use a break-even analysis after the cost and income functions have changed.

CONTROLLED GROWTH

Once you have an established solid customer base and a good cash flow, set the right measured pace for your business. Some indications that an expansion may be warranted include the inability to fill customer needs efficiently or employees having difficulty keeping up with production demands.

If expansion is warranted, after careful review, research and analysis, identify what and who you need to add in order for your business to grow. Then, with the right systems and people in place, you can focus on the growth of your business, not on doing everything in it yourself. Remember, most self-made millionaires possess average intelligence; what sets them apart is their openness to new knowledge and their willingness to learn whatever it takes to succeed.

You'll Make $ERIOUS
MONEY Online!

Chapter Thirteen

Establishing a Niche

REASON FOR FAILURE #5
FAILURE TO ESTABLISH A NICHE

There's only one way left to make serious money online… find a niche.

A niche is simply a specific subject matter that your business focuses on. A niche allows you, a small business, to compete with big businesses. Big businesses have more money, more resources and more staff than you do. They can drive much more traffic and spend lots more money on branding their business in the mind of consumers. With a niche you are able to compete with big businesses – by delivering the precise products, service and (just as importantly) the information, that fulfils the specific needs of your niche market.

THE MORE YOU TELL, THE MORE YOU SELL

Research proves that the more information you provide (i) the more people will buy from you, (ii) the conversion rate of those prospects will increase, (iii) each sale will cost you less (through reduced advertising costs) and (iv) you'll take customers away from your competitors.

> "Knowledge is power."
> Francis Bacon

More people will buy from you because more people are likely to find you during a search engine search for the information you are providing about your product or service, which they are interested in. Also, the more information about your product or service you provide, the more trust you engender in your prospect.

If you are perceived by your prospect to have more knowledge of your product or service than your competitors, then your prospect will perceive you to be an 'expert' regarding the product or service you are providing. Because the prospect will trust you more, and perceive less risk in any consequent purchase, your sales conversion rate will also increase.

Information reduces your advertising costs because you'll intercept prospects at an earlier stage in the search funnel. When an Internet user is interested in finding information regarding a subject, product or service, obviously they search for it. Most users start with a generic term (e.g. 'cameras'). If they don't find what they are looking for, they then refine their search (e.g. 'sports cameras'). If, again, they don't find what they are looking for, they will refine their search, usually for the last time (e.g. 'waterproof sports cameras').

If that user had found a website with the information they were looking for (i.e. 'waterproof sports cameras') in their first search, then they would not have had to look through any competitors' websites. Therefore, this proves that the more relevant information you can provide about your product or service (i.e. all related products, the industry, the process of manufacture, its history etc.), then the more likely you are to capture prospects.

Also, by 'educating' the visitor on everything they would possibly want to know about the product or service they are interested in, it allows you to significantly reduce your sponsored links advertising costs (e.g. Google Sponsored Links). This is because you'll be able to advertise using the cheaper 'generic' keywords, key phrases and search terms (e.g. 'cameras') rather than the more expensive 'specific' ones (e.g. 'waterproof digital cameras').

The more information you provide for your prospect, the less likely they are to look elsewhere for information. If you provide every answer to every question the prospect has regarding your product or service, why should they look elsewhere? Therefore, it also cuts out your competitors; because once you have captured your prospect's attention and provided them with everything they need, and proved your expertise, they are 87% less likely to visit a competitor website.

Once you have chosen your niche, and provided as much information as possible, you should also create a unique proposition strategy that fulfills a need of your niche audience.

You'll Make $ERIOUS
MONEY Online!

Chapter Fourteen

Creating a Unique Proposition Strategy

REASON FOR FAILURE #6
FAILURE TO CREATE A UNIQUE
PROPOSITION STRATEGY

Your business' *Unique Proposition Strategy*™ (UPS) should include at least the following elements:

1. Unique Selling Proposition (USP)
2. Unique Value Proposition (UVP)
3. Unique Tactical Plan (UTP)

WITHOUT A UPS, YOU'LL BE IN A MESS!

In terms of establishing a successful business, **a UPS is second only in importance to establishing a profitable niche**.

Why should your customers buy from you and not your competition? To find out, evaluate your business for what makes it unique and attractive for your customers. Then, summarize your key selling points that make your product or service a 'must have' for your clients. If you don't have a UPS get one!

The most important part of a Unique Proposition Strategy is the Unique Selling Proposition. Therefore, always emphasize your USP in your promotions and marketing. It is your USP that will attract prospects to your business, rather than your competition. Do you offer a much needed personalized service, or customized solutions, or shorter turnaround time, or after sales service?

Do you know what your Unique Value Proposition is?

"Price is what you pay. Value is what you get."
Warren Buffett

You can formulate your UVP through depth of thought and rigorous analysis of your product or service's market place, competition and existing practices. It involves listening to what your customers are saying, understanding their needs and then providing exactly what they want.

> "The aim of marketing is to know and understand the customer so well that the product or service fits him and sells itself."
>
> Peter Drucker

Typical UVPs include customized solutions, customer loyalty schemes and added value offers such as free products, services and bonuses. Make sure your business offers something that customers would value.

> "If there is any one secret of success, it lies in the ability to get the other person's point of view and see things from that person's angle as well as from your own."
>
> Henry Ford

What is your Unique Tactical Plan (UTP)? How will you present and deliver your USP and UVP?

UPS is the overall strategy, UTP is the individual tactics. You may require multiple strategic plans and tactics to fulfill your commitment to your customer. For example, a pizza company may have a USP that promises pizzas delivered in 30 minutes and a UVP of discounting money off a customer's next pizza. The UTP required to fulfill these propositions would be hand-delivered pizzas using cars and high speed scooters and money off coupons with every delivery.

If your niche is selling underwater digital cameras online you may have the USP of offering free, unlimited after-sales service and a UVP of offering money off diving vacations. Your UTP will require a toll free phone number to fulfill your USP proposition and an emailed printable coupon to fulfill your UVP proposition. You should continue to plan more unique tactics to further promote your products or services and extend your competitive advantage.

"Strategy without tactics is the slowest route to victory.
Tactics without strategy is the noise before defeat."
Sun Tzu

You'll Make $ERIOUS
MONEY Online!

Chapter Fifteen

Building Long-Term Value

REASON FOR FAILURE #7
FAILURE TO BUILD LONG-TERM VALUE

Focusing on short-term profits rather than building long-term value is a short-sighted business strategy. It's important to be profitable, but not when short-term profits come at the expense of the long-term value of the business and the lifetime value of each customer.

For example, imagine you sell a product that uses expensive parts or ingredients. You can cut your costs by reducing the quality of those parts or ingredients and your profits will grow temporarily, but your customers will notice and stop buying it. Saving a few dollars today will cost you big in the long run.

A CUSTOMER IS FOR LIFE, NOT JUST FOR CHRISTMAS

The 'lifetime value' of a customer refers to the entire amount of money earned from that customer over the entire time they are part of your customer base; their entire 'value' to you as a customer rather than just the profit made from them from a single one-off sale.

> "All lasting business is built on friendship."
> Alfred A. Montapert

Rather than concentrating on single, one-off sales, a long-term, sustainable business model should be based on creating a sizeable community of loyal customers and repeat buyers. It is through this loyal community that your word-of-mouth sales will come and upon which your company's goodwill and reputation will be built.

> "If you do build a great experience, customers tell each other about that. Word of mouth is very powerful."
> Jeff Bezos

There's an old saying in marketing, 'The money is in the list'. This advice refers to the fact that it is more profitable to keep working your customer database and marketing to your established customers through direct customer contact (direct marketing) than to try to attract new customers.

> "There is only one boss. The customer. And he can fire everybody in the company from the chairman on down, simply by spending his money somewhere else."
> Sam Walton

The Customer Life Cycle:

1. Attract the customer
2. Make the sale
3. Capture the customer's contact details
4. 1st Direct Customer Contact – 'Thank you' page and receipt
5. 2nd Direct Customer Contact – Regularly notify customer of special offers etc.
6. 3rd Direct Customer Contact – Answering questions and resolving problems
7. 4th Direct Customer Contact – Invite them to join your 'community' (e.g. blog)
8. 5th Direct Customer Contact – Invite them to 'Tell a Friend' about you
9. Make repeat sale
10. Repeat the cycle.

THE PARETO PRINCIPLE (THE 80/20 RULE)

Attracting new customers is expensive (depending on your advertising costs), whereas advertising to an existing customer can be very cheap (e.g. email, face-to-face, or phone communication).

Considering that 20% of your customers buy 80% of your products, it is always the better sales strategy to try to keep your existing customers happy (e.g. through added value bonuses and 'privileged customer' special offers etc.) than to spend limited advertising budgets on attracting new customers or speculative campaigns.

> "Profit in business comes from repeat customers, customers that boast about your project or service, and that bring friends with them."
>
> W. Edwards Deming

Try to identify hyper-responsive customers and try to turn each of these fans into a maven, that will recommend your product or service to prospects through word-of-mouth or viral marketing, to attract more customers rather than trying to attract new customers outside your target market that are much less likely to want your product or service.

You'll Make $ERIOUS
MONEY Online!

Chapter Sixteen

World Class Marketing

REASON FOR FAILURE #8
POOR MARKETING

Failing to position your marketing correctly, or failing to adapt to a changing market (e.g. being out of touch with customers), or failure to market online without using techniques such as the *Keyword Continuum*™, will break your business.

As you know, there are hundreds of thousands of websites out there, so you have to continually promote your website to let people know that you exist. If people don't know your website is out there they are certainly not going to find it by chance.

> "The wheel that squeaks the loudest is the one that gets the grease."
>
> Josh Billings

To succeed online you need great marketing that continually promotes your website. If you are caught up in handling the everyday operations of your business (i.e. "firefighting" instead of progressing) and neglect your marketing, you'll quickly have no business at all.

MARKETING IS EVERYTHING

A lack of marketing expertise can severely restrict your business' success and development. Your customers won't buy from you if they don't know you exist; you need to market yourself. However, always make your marketing message consistent and true to your brand.

> "Every advertisement should be thought of as a
> contribution to the complex symbol which is the
> brand image."
>
> David Ogilvy

Don't make the mistake of treating marketing as an unnecessary expense, but remember that it can be a huge waste of money if not targeted properly. Find cost effective ways to market yourself through advertising, direct marketing, trade shows and exhibitions. Set up your website and market yourself through Internet media such as blogs, forums, email groups and search engine marketing. Always base your advertising on your real world research.

> "Advertising people who ignore research are as
> dangerous as generals who ignore decodes of
> enemy signals."
>
> David Ogilvy

The results are never instant and you need to find the optimum mix that works for your industry. Hire a consultant if you don't have the expertise in-house.

The Five Ps of Marketing

1. **Product**
2. **Person**
3. **Price**
4. **Place**
5. **Position**

Product – the product's benefits and features (i.e. what the product can do for the customer)

Person – the target customer/market (i.e. the person the product will benefit most or is most likely to buy the product)

Price – the optimal price for which the product can be sold (i.e. the price at which the seller will sell most units)

Place – the channel to market (i.e. the best way to sell the most units to the most customers – Internet, bricks-and-mortar shop, door-to-door selling etc.)

Position – the level in the market at which the product will be sold (i.e. positioned to appeal to the 'high end' premium-price sector, the mid-price market sector, or the 'low end', low-price, 'tack 'em high 'n' sell 'em cheap' sector).

NEVER COMPETE ON PRICE

Many experienced entrepreneurs make it a rule never to launch a business in a new market unless they can compete at the high end, and most experienced business owners will advise you never to compete on price.

Even though the Internet is a marketplace where consumers expect to get the best deals, customers that buy on price are not loyal; the 'lifetime of the customer' (the total sales made to that customer) can be limited to just one sale, thus significantly reducing the chances of you making a meaningful profit from this type of customer.

Another reason why it is risky to base your business model on providing products and services at a low price is that it is easy to underestimate the true total cost of your product or service. When you start your business you'll probably do most, if not all, of the work yourself. However, when you employ other people to do the same work you'll have to calculate the cost of the work they do, the time it takes to do that work and the taxes, benefits, insurance etc.

Therefore, it is essential to evaluate the real cost of breaking even (see BREAK-EVEN POINT CALCULATION, Chapter Twelve). Although you may attract more customers with your low prices you may not make enough money to cover all costs and become profitable.

NEEDS, WANTS AND EGOS

"You now have to decide what 'image' you want for your
brand. Image means personality. Products, like people,
have personalities, and they can make or break them in
the market place."

David Ogilvy

Any market has three price positions; the highest price, middle
price and lowest price. You'll probably feel most comfortable
positioning your product or service in the middle price range;
however, this is where most of your competition will probably
be and, consequently, it will be difficult to stand out from the
crowd.

My advice is to always try to be at the top end of any
market; it is easier to add value (higher quality, bonuses,
guarantees, warranties, better after-sales service, customer
care, add-on products and services etc.) to a product or service
and charge a higher price than to sell very high quantities of a
product at low margin, low prices, to make a profit. Also,
because the margins are so low, you'll have to be a better
business person to compete, as any mistake with your pricing
strategy could put you out of business.

"Anybody can cut prices, but it takes brains to make a
better article."

Philip Armour

The low end, low price segment of any market attracts
unfaithful, transitory, bargain-seeking customers that will be
hard to re-sell to, so will not have any significant lifetime value
to you. Besides, there will always be someone that will lower
their price to undercut you, and in that situation only the
customer wins.

PRICING STRATEGIES

Your pricing strategy will depend on (i) how you decide to position your product or service, (ii) the customers you are targeting, and (iii) the profit objectives you have set.

Your price strategy should take into account factors such as your company's overall marketing objectives, consumer demand, product attributes, competitors' pricing, and market and economic trends. There are many ways to price a product with an optimum strategy for every objective.

Penetration Pricing

This strategy demands that the price charged for your product or service is set artificially low in order to gain a large market share. Once this is achieved, the price is increased. This strategy is very often used by subscription-based services, such as telecoms and TV companies.

Price Skimming

This strategy is used when you charge a high price because you have a substantial competitive advantage; although the advantage may not be sustainable. The high price tends to attract new competitors into the market, and the price inevitably falls due to increased supply. Manufacturers of new digital products (e.g. flat screen TVs) use this skimming strategy. Once other manufacturers enter the market and the products are produced at a lower unit cost, other marketing and pricing strategies are implemented.

Premium Pricing

You may choose to use premium prices when there is a uniqueness or exclusivity about your product or service. This strategy is used where a substantial competitive advantage exists. Such high prices are used for aspirational luxury products and services such as designer products or first class services, such as hotel accommodation or travel.

Economy Pricing

This is a "no frills", low price strategy, where the cost of marketing and manufacture are kept at a minimum.

Supermarkets often use this strategy for their own economy branded everyday essentials such as milk, bread and eggs.

Note: Premium pricing, penetration pricing, economy pricing, and price skimming are four of the most popular pricing strategies. However, there are other important strategies to pricing.

Psychological Pricing

This strategy is used when the marketer wants the consumer to respond on an emotional, rather than rational, logical basis. For example, using the 'price point perspective' e.g. $9.99 cents rather than $10.

Product Line Pricing

This pricing strategy is used where there is a range of products or services, and the pricing reflects the benefits of parts of the range. For example, in a service industry: basic service $24.99, standard service $49.99, and premier service $99.99.

Captive Product Pricing

If you sell products that have complimentary goods, you can charge a premium price once the prospect is converted into a customer. For example, if you sell a printer you can charge a low price and recoup your margin (and more) from the sale of the only ink cartridge which is compatible with that printer. A famous example of this strategy was used over a hundred years ago by Smith & Wesson, who used to give their handguns away knowing that their customers had to use their ammunition.

Optional Product Pricing

Using this strategy companies try to increase the total amount each customer spends after those customers have made an initial purchase. This is often done by using optional 'extras' to increase the overall prices of the product or service. For example, companies will charge for optional extras such as product warrantees, discounted upgrades, or express delivery.

Promotional Pricing
Pricing to promote a product is a very common strategy. There are many examples of promotional pricing including strategies such as 'Buy One Get One Free', '3 for the price of 2', 'Special Offer', 'Limited Offers' etc.

Product Bundle Pricing
Sellers use this strategy to combine several products in the same package. This strategy also serves to move old stock. Downloadable digital products are often sold using the bundle strategy.

Geographical Pricing
Geographical pricing is used where there are variations in price in different parts of the world. Influencing factors include: rarity value, or where shipping costs increase price.

Value Pricing
This strategy is used where external factors, such as recession, or increased competition, force companies to provide 'value' products and services to help people afford their products and so retain sales (e.g. value meals at McDonalds).

ARE YOUR CUSTOMERS SPENDING MONEY?

If you can't find anyone able to sell to your target market, this may be a warning sign that your potential customers aren't willing to spend money for your product or service.

Competition is good – it proves people want to buy the product or service you want to sell. Ideally, you want a limited number of competition and sufficient niches in that sector to exploit.

Remember, you'll be selling a "benefit" not a product or service. If your customers can get the same benefit from a better, cheaper, quicker, alternative to your product or service then they will desert you. As new, alternative products and services come along so you should adapt and not be left behind – provide whatever your customer requires.

> "We see our customers as invited guests to a party, and
> we are the hosts. It's our job every day to make every
> important aspect of the customer experience a little bit
> better."
>
> Jeff Bezos

HYPER-RESPONSIVE CUSTOMERS

Identifying which customers are hyper-responsive, rather than just responsive, is often the difference between moderate success and massive success.

> "In marketing I've seen only one strategy that can't miss –
> and that is to market to your best customers first, your
> best prospects second and the rest of the world last."
>
> John Romero

Obviously, clues to finding potentially hyper-responsive customers can be found in your order book or database, but also include the willingness to provide their personal phone number in a survey; if they are committed enough to go offline to communicate with you then they are much more likely to be a responsive customer.

NICHE-BASED STRATEGY

To dominate your chosen niche you'll have to thoroughly understand all the subgroups you discover through your research and understand any new niche markets better than any competitors before you waste your precious resources on them; even before you ever develop a product or service.

"Determine what your customers need and work backward."
Jeff Bezos

The secret to dominating the niche you choose is to then create an extremely tight message-to-market match so that your prospects and customers are satisfied that what you are offering is exactly what they were looking for.

This kind of market research very often reveals that what most business people think is only one market is very often really multiple niche segments of potential customers with distinctly different needs.

THE SEARCH FUNNEL

Your research will help you learn how people tend to move from one keyword to the next as they become more involved in your product or service. This 'funnel' of search terms, keywords and key phrases will help you discover exactly what prospects are searching for and help you refine your marketing message as well as decide exactly which products, services and (just as importantly) what information they are searching for.

This research will help you decide on the *Keyword Continuum*™ you should use when developing your search funnel or sales funnel. The aim is also to empathize with your customers so you can become a trusted information resource and advisor. If you provide sufficient information, and reach this level of trust, then customers are much less likely to turn to your competition.

"The more informative your advertising, the more persuasive it will be."

David Ogilvy

Chapter Seventeen

Product Strategy

REASON FOR FAILURE #9
POOR PRODUCT STRATEGY

Don't try to reinvent the wheel when it comes to products or services. You are more likely to lose money than to make it. Instead, choose a popular market and identify a niche within it that you can dominate quickly.

Choose your products carefully and try to sell what you understand. Where possible, find something you're passionate about and build a business out of that. The most successful online websites are the niche websites such as special interest websites built around specific themes. Initially, affiliate programs may be a good way to start your online business, but selling or producing your own product should be in your future plans if you want real Internet success.

IF IT'S GOOD, IT'S GOOD

Whatever your core product, service or competence is, stick to it. Coca Cola is over 100 years old and attracts more and more customers worldwide every day. If it's good, it's good. If it's bad, we make excuses.

Research, and real-life examples, prove that it's better to (i) keep improving on a good product or service (i.e. reduce costs, improve packaging, delivery and customer service etc.) and (ii) concentrate on "brand extension", rather than to diversify into totally different markets.

> "There are two kinds of companies, those that work to try to charge more and those that work to charge less. We will be the second."
>
> Jeff Bezos

An excellent example of brand extension would be recent diversification of chocolate bars such as Snickers or Mars into markets such as ice cream or 'fun size' miniature bars or Easter eggs. It's essentially the same product (i.e. the same ingredients, packaging design, and taste) but it is aimed at different market sectors.

Brand extension works because people's recognition of the brand reassures them about the product's quality (they know what it should taste like even before they buy it) and it's the presentation (small 'bite size' portions for kids or ice cream bars for hot days) that compels people to use the same product but in different forms and in different environments on different occasions.

The intention of brand extension is to use the same product or service but market it in a way that will appeal to different people at different times, thus extending its potential customer base and sales. Think about how you could diversify into a related market sectors by extending your product or service.

Ultimately, similar to Coca Cola's expansion strategy, it is better to try to attract new customers than to produce new, potentially competitive products.

Note: Brand extension is a totally different strategy to "line extension", which refers to when a line of different new products are produced alongside an established product. If these new products are produced for the same target market they can become a competitive product to your core products, which can cannibalize your sales and attract substantial start-up costs as well as divert your resources away from your core competence.

QUALITY = ATTENTION TO DETAIL

If you are going to position your product or service at the top end of any market then you'll have to offer your prospects something different, or more for their money, than your competitors. Simply improving the design of your product or service is often the answer.

> "Almost all quality improvement comes via simplification of design, manufacturing... layout, processes, and procedures."
>
> Tom Peters

At the high end of any market are fewer customers. This is because there are always fewer people prepared to spend more money for something that they can get for less money elsewhere.

At the high end of any market are the discerning customers who are prepared to pay more because they put a higher value on that product or service. This may be because the product or service is more beneficial to them than others (e.g. a good quality waterproof camera might be invaluable to a keen scuba diver but of no significance whatsoever to another person).

Very often, high end products, such as 'designer' goods, achieve a perceived value that is far beyond their intrinsic value, due to their 'aspirational' appeal. For example, $1,000 handbags and shoes are priced far beyond their real value (Chinese labor and Indian leather is not that expensive) but because they appeal to their target customer's aspirations and wants, rather than actual needs, they can be priced at an extremely profitable level.

> "If advertisers spent the same amount of money on improving their products as they do on advertising then they wouldn't have to advertise them."
>
> Will Rogers

Ideally, this is what you would aim to achieve; leveraging a higher perceived value for your product or service through market positioning, branding and advertising, rather than producing more costly goods or services.

At the high end of any market people will pay for quality. By quality, I mean attention to detail. It's these 'details' for which people will pay extra. Details can be the finish of a product (e.g. the lining of a suit or handbag), or for digital products this is often provided through the added-value products or services that come with the product (e.g. high quality information). Consistently producing high quality products and services is a major key to prolonged success.

> "Quality is not an act, it is a habit."
>
> Aristotle

Two Brands Are Better Than One

Never try to be all things to all people. If you have products that you want to advertise to different segments of the same market, then use two separate brands. I can only think of one brand (Tesco, UK) that has ever been able to appeal to multiple levels of the same market.

All other brands have had to create a new brand when marketing a different product to a different target market at a different market position (e.g. Toyota's 'Lexus' executive cars and Nokia's 'Vertu' premium phones). Therefore, if you want to split your products, you'd better split your target marketing too.

Feedback

Most small businesses are able to have a personal relationship with customers. This is one advantage that huge corporations don't have. You need to focus on good quality products and services and aim at attaining high customer satisfaction levels.

> "Your most unhappy customers are your greatest source
> of learning."
>
> Bill Gates

Use customer feedback as free business advice. Ask you customers for feedback and suggestions, then evaluate them and incorporate the findings into your business. This mechanism can help you gauge changes in your customers' tastes, preferences, price sensitivity etc. This may also be the best source of information about your competitor's activities. Feedback will help you avoid adding new products or divisions to your operation that may drag down your already profitable ones and avoid you falling out of touch with your customers.

BUILDING BARRIERS

The cheaper it is to start a business the more competition it is likely to attract. Therefore, the more likely it is to fail; due to that business's "low barriers to entry". Some barriers to entry include:

- Cost
- Intellectual Property
- Brand Recognition
- Skills and Experience
- Added Value

Due to the lower set-up costs, Internet businesses are particularly susceptible to competitors entering their markets, and having successful business models copied.

The best way to build barriers around your business, and prevent competitors entering your business sector, is to be the best in your sector. Therefore, try to be the biggest, most recognizable and trusted brand in your sector. Provide the best product, best service, and best customer service you possibly can, then provide as much 'added value' to your products or services as possible.

> "The man who will use his skill and constructive
> imagination to see how *much* he can give for a dollar,
> instead of how *little* he can give for a dollar, is bound
> to succeed."
>
> Henry Ford

IS IT SCALABLE?

What if your business takes off immediately? Could you handle 1,000s of orders every day? The most successful businesses are the ones that are 'scalable' and not dependent on any one element. Once you develop a workable, profitable and efficient business model and processes that are scalable, you can then consider rolling out the same model into different markets; providing different products and services using the same proven model. This is so much easier online because most of the model and processes will be automated software that can be easily configured to fit a new product or service.

DEPENDENT UPON THE NUMBER OF USERS?

Many online business models, such as matchmaking services, community and forum-based businesses, are based on attaining a 'critical mass' (i.e. specific large number) of users or members, or 'network effects' (i.e. the large number of users providing the reason for using the service). For this type of business model to succeed it requires a large number of active users.

For such a business to succeed it is imperative to research and calculate precisely how much it will cost you to market and promote such a service until it becomes profitable. You will also have to provide the content necessary to entertain your users until your users can provide the content necessary themselves. 'Positives Dating', (PART TWO: DON'T RE-INVENT THE WHEEL!), is a good example of an online business model based on network effects.

CREATE YOUR OWN COMPETITOR

I know this is controversial, but it is now a well-used online tactic to defend a sector-leading position in a new, niche, market sector from copycat competitors; creating your own 'competitor'.

> "The supreme art of war is to subdue the enemy
> without fighting."
>
> Sun Tzu

Every market has two major competitors (e.g. McDonalds/Burger King, Apple/Microsoft, Pepsi/Coke) and any company wanting to compete in the industries dominated by these brands needs to take on not one but two established brands.

You might have a chance of competing against one established brand in one sector, but with two? Unlikely. That's why many clever Internet-based companies develop a rival company to (i) appeal to the other potential customers not targeted by the original business and (ii) put off potential competitors from ever entering their sector.

This tactic is particularly useful when defending the top position of in PPC advertising.

> "Victorious warriors win first and then go to war,
> while defeated warriors go to war first and then seek
> to win."
>
> Sun Tzu

You'll Make $ERIOUS
MONEY Online!

Chapter Eighteen

Establishing a Team

REASON FOR FAILURE #10
FAILURE TO ESTABLISH A TEAM

"The whole is more than the sum of its parts."
Aristotle

Are you doing all of the work in your business yourself? If you are, you need to re-evaluate. Nearly every successful entrepreneur has a support system or advisor or a mentor of some kind. In fact, very often an entrepreneur uses the time and money of others to make his ideas a reality.

"Hire people who are better than you are, then leave
them to get on with it. Look for people who will aim for
the remarkable, who will not settle for the routine."
David Ogilvy

Too many small business people are caught up in doing the day-to-day 'fire-fighting' of running their businesses. As a result, they are unable to work on the bigger picture of growing their businesses.

"Hardly any human being is capable of pursuing
two professions or two arts rightly."
Plato

You have to stop trying to be your own copy writer, web designer, customer support staff, product innovator, tax accountant, marketer, search engine optimizer, press release contact, book keeper, etc., etc., etc..

"Teamwork is so important that it is virtually impossible for
you to reach the heights of your capabilities or make the
money that you want without becoming very good at it."
Brian Tracy

Start becoming a believer in the saying, "Do what you do best and farm out the rest!"

> "The best teamwork comes from men who are
> working independently toward one goal in unison."
>> James Cash Penney

Establish a "team" of people who help you succeed. Some will work with you and/or for you. Others will be mentors to you. Use your team to help build your business and improve your prosperity.

> "If everyone is moving forward together, then success takes
> care of itself."
>> Henry Ford

You Should Not Be The Business

> "A company is only as good as the people it keeps."
>> Mary Kay Ash

Your business should be built to operate without you. You should be managing the work, not doing it, and concentrate on growing the business. You should be looking to employ staff to do every part of the business process as quickly as you can afford it.

> "I am looking for a lot of men who have an infinite capacity
> to not know what can't be done."
>> Henry Ford

Most businesses can be separated into three distinct centers; for example: marketing, production and distribution. Therefore, if the business is a success, you'll eventually need to employ someone for each process.

"All things will be produced in superior quantity and quality, and with greater ease, when each man works at a single occupation, in accordance with his natural gifts, and at the right moment, without meddling with anything else."
Plato

Once you employ someone you have to train them, and every subsequent employee, to do the job exactly the same way as you would like it done. To achieve this, everything needs to be broken down into procedures, through "process mapping"; the series of steps required to conduct a process.

Because the time will come when you'll want to sell the business. Therefore, even if your business is a consultancy you should consider calling it something other than your name and avoiding the business revolving around you and depending on what you do personally. Otherwise, no one will buy the business without you attached!

Note: Business Process Mapping refers to activities involved in defining exactly what a business entity does, who is responsible, to what standard a process should be completed and how the success of a business process can be determined. For example, ISO 9001 requires a business entity to follow a 'process approach' when managing its business.

OUTSOURCING

Depending on your business model, it is very often good advice to outsource every non-essential function. Many businesses now outsource every part of their business functions other than its unique in-house skills. This keeps down their costs and opens up a huge potential pool of resources and a much higher skills level.

"I only want people around me who can do the impossible."
Elizabeth Arden

STRATEGIC SYNERGY

Using *Strategic Synergy*™, such as partnerships, affiliate schemes, and other cooperative selling campaigns can significantly improve your sales.

"In sales, a referral is the key to the door of resistance."
Bo Bennett

There are many good online affiliate schemes; giving you access to thousands of potential affiliates willing to help sell your product or service for a commission fee.

PLATE 51: AFFILIATE PARTNER WEBSITE

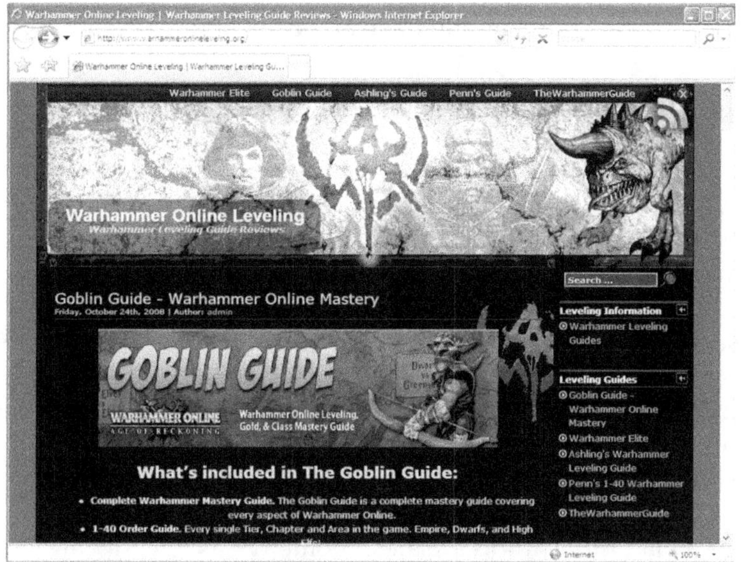

Alternatively, try to find strategic partners that already sell to your target market. Ideally, try to find a partner that produces a complimentary (non-competitive) product or service to your own. For example, if you produce ladies handbags then try to partner with someone that produces ladies shoes. If you sell underwater digital cameras then try to partner with a holiday specialist, travel agent or scuba diving brand.

> "Affiliate marketing has made businesses millions and ordinary people millionaires."
> Bo Bennett

Sharing each other's customer database, as well as introducing and recommending each other's products or services, can significantly increase your sales and can prove extremely beneficial to both parties.

And now, the moment you have all been waiting for…

THE $MILLION SECRET

Take your online business offline! That's right; add an offline sales department. People like to talk to people, and they like to see and interact with people; social networking websites have proved this anthropological fact beyond doubt.

Also, the most efficient way of selling anything to someone else is to do it face-to-face. That's why successful Internet-based businesses that integrate their successful online business model with an offline sales operation invariably increase their sales immeasurably.

By 'offline sales operation' I mean any person-to-person, sales-orientated communication, such as telesales follow-ups, 'live chat', door-to-door sales, home visits etc. I can give several examples of 'me too', also ran, Internet-based businesses that added an offline sales division to their business model and became million dollar revenue-earning businesses within 12 months. Try it for yourself, as soon as your online business is profitable.

CONCLUSION

There's only one way left for most small business people to make serious money online. To help ensure that your online business is a successful one, it is vitally important to target a profitable niche. Those are the pots of gold hidden in the Internet that can make you $ERIOUS MONEY!

Good Luck!

Dr Richard G. Lewis
www.riskeliminator.com

P.S. Sign up for my FREE Newsletter to enjoy many more tips on making $ERIOUS MONEY Online!

You'll Make $ERIOUS MONEY Online!

CHECKLIST

1. Try to find a business that you would actually enjoy running.
2. Sell things that appeal to people's needs and wants.
3. Use a business model that has the *Strategic Fit*™ for the Internet.
4. Don't be a vanguard unless you have the money to pay for the support system that is required for any new product or service. Instead, identify a niche within a larger, already successful market sector.
5. Use the *Risk Eliminator*™ to identify, test and/or research niche markets.
6. Copy successful online businesses.
7. Develop a *Unique Proposition Strategy*™.
8. Use *Strategic Synergy*™ to develop your business.
9. Use the *Keyword Continuum*™ to market your business online, and add an integrated sales department offline.
10. Build barriers to entry and create your own competitor!

You'll Make $ERIOUS
MONEY Online!

GLOSSARY

56Kbps
This is the speed at which a 56Kbps modem will run. 56Kbps is the minimum speed modem available. The faster the speed, the quicker you'll be able to download web pages etc.

Access Provider
The company (also called an Internet service provider or ISP) that sells access and provides the method of connecting customers to the Internet.

Ad Group
A Google Ad Group (advertising group) contains one or more advertisements that target a specific set of keywords, placements, or both, related to a group of your choosing.

Affiliate Program (Affiliate Scheme)
An affiliate is typically paid a commission from the company they are affiliated to for reselling products or providing services produced by that company. A corporation or person may be referred to as an affiliate of another when it is related to it but not strictly controlled by it, as with a subsidiary relationship, or when it wishes to avoid the appearance of being controlled by another company.

Aggregate Information
Aggregate information is information presented in summary or statistical form that does not contain data that would identify a specific individual on his or her own.

Blogs
A blog (short for 'web log') is a type of website diary with regular entries of descriptions.

Brand Extension
Also known as 'brand sweating', is the diversification of a brand into a different but still closely related market sector.

Bandwidth
This is used to explain how much data can be sent through a connection to the Net. Typically, text files use little bandwidth, while pictures and sound files use much more. This digital traffic is measured in bits per second, so a modem running at 57,600bps is twice as fast as one at 28,800bps. The term has been copied from electronics, where bandwidth is used to measure in kilohertz (KHz) or megahertz (MHz) the frequency at which analogue devices carry electronic signals.

Browser
A software application that allows browsing of the Internet.

Cannibalize
To "Cannibalize" is to deprive one business, or part of a business, or business' function, of vital elements or resources, such as personnel, equipment, or funding, for use elsewhere. It can also mean to divert income from one business or revenue from a specific product or service at the expense of another.

Core Competence
A company's *Core Competence* is something that the company executes well across several business units or product sectors, compared to its competitors.

Cost Per Click
This is the cost to you for every time each prospect clicks on your ad.

Cookies
A "cookie" (also browser cookie, tracking cookie, and HTTP cookie) is a small string of text data stored on a user's computer by a web browser. Some websites place a cookie on your computer when you visit it. This is done so that if you return to the website, it will be able to read the cookie to see what you did last visit and add more information.

Database
A PC filing cabinet for data with some powerful searching capabilities.

Dialogue Box
A window, which pops up to give you information, or requires you to input information.

DNS
Domain Name System. The system that regulates the naming of website addresses on the Internet.

Domain Names
A Domain Name defines the IP Address of a website and the ownership of that website. The domain name forms the latter part of a URL (e.g. sony.com in the URL http://www.sony.com). It is also used in email addresses (e.g. name@sony.com). Without domain names users would have to type in IP numbers to connect to other computers on the Internet.

Download
The act of taking information or applications from the World Wide Web and storing it on a computer's hard disk.

Drop Shipping
Drop shipping is a supply chain management technique in which the retailer does not keep goods in stock, but instead transfers customer orders and shipment details to either the manufacturer or a wholesaler, who then ships the goods directly to the customer.

E-Commerce
Electronic commerce (e-commerce) is a general concept that covers any form of business transaction that is conducted electronically using telecommunications networks, including the Internet.

Economies of Scale
Economies of scale refers to reductions in unit cost as the size of a facility, or scale, increases and the factors that cause a producer's average cost per unit to fall as scale is increased.

E-mail
Short for "electronic mail": a means of sending and receiving messages via the Internet.

E-mail Address
The unique address which allows people to send e-mail.

Encryption
A method of coding data to prevent unauthorized access, most commonly used on the Net to protect e-mail or credit card transactions.

FAQs
Frequently Asked Questions. An FAQ file is a compilation of questions and answers listed on a website that helps newcomers to that website.

Firefighting
Frantically dealing with everyday business problems, administration, processes and functions.

Firewall
Basically a piece of hardware or software that sits between a Web server and a standalone computer or corporate network so that those who log onto the Web server cannot also access another computer or a company's network without permission.

File
Any whole piece of data stored on your computer; e.g. a program or a document.

FTP (File Transfer Protocol)
File Transfer Protocol is a technology that allows data to be transferred across the Net. Although most browsers include FTP support the best option is for a company to equip itself with an FTP program such as Cute FTP from www.cuteftp.com.

Gb
A thousand megabytes. A measurement of the storage space of a hard disk.

Google.com
Google is a major Internet search engine. Google Inc. is an American public corporation, earning revenue from advertising related to its Internet search, e-mail, online mapping, office productivity, social networking, and video sharing services as well as selling advertising-free versions of the same technologies.

Homepage
The opening/introduction page of a website (not necessarily the 'landing page', which can be any on a website that a user visits first).

Host
A computer on the Internet that allows users to connect to it to access files, such as a website.

HTML
A derivative of the Standard Graphical Mark Up Language (SGML), HyperText Markup Language (HTML) is the language used to create Web pages. The simple text formatting and linking commands can be created in a text editor although programs such as *HTML Pro* from SoftQuad, *Pagemill* from Adobe and *Internet Assistant* for Word from Microsoft make the whole thing simple.

HTTP
Hyper Text Transfer Protocol. The normal way of transferring HTML documents between servers and browsers.

Hyper-Responsive Customer
Hyper-responsive customers are those customers that are exceptionally responsive to offers. Typically, a business might generate a very high percentage of its income from a very small percentage of its customers; these are the hyper-responsive customers.

Hypertext Link
A key feature of the Web is that HTML allows documents anywhere on the Web to link to each another by clicking on links (see Link).

Hub
Computers which tie other computers together to allow them to combine their memory and work together to process information beyond their individual capacity.

Intellectual Property (IP)
Intellectual property is the legal property rights over creations of the mind, both artistic and commercial, and the corresponding fields of law (e.g. trademarks etc.).

Internet (or Net)
An international network that links thousands of computers, using telephone and cable links.

IP (Internet Protocol)
Internet Protocol allows data to be stored in packets that can be sent across multiple networks to an address, which is usually in the form of an IP number. Each individual computer on the Internet has an IP number. Dial-up customers are dynamically given IP addresses every time they log on; allowing them to behave as if they were permanently connected to the network.

IP Address
The unique numeric address of a computer on the Internet.

ISP (Internet Service Provider)
An Internet Service Provider is an organization from which access to the Internet can be bought. AOL, MSN, and CompuServe are some of the biggest names in the USA and EU.

Java
Perhaps the most significant Internet technology of recent years, Java was developed by Sun (www.sun.com). Java is a

programming language that allows tiny programs, or applets, to be created and sent over a network (e.g. the Internet). Initially, much Java development led to simple animations and games but more compelling uses are now starting to appear.

JIT (just-in-time)
JIT is an inventory strategy implemented to improve the return on investment of a business by reducing in-process inventory and its associated carrying costs.

Keywords
A word used by a search engine in its search for relevant Web pages.

Keyword Continuum
The *Keyword Continuum*™ is the directive that you should use the same keyword or key phrase that the user originally searched for, or clicked on, throughout your website's whole click-through path, search funnel, or sales funnel.

KPIs (Key Performance Indicators)
Key Performance Indicators are quantifiable measurements, agreed to and set before an action, that reflects the critical success factors of an action or process. These are often used in business to measure the success of a business.

Landing Page
In online marketing a "landing page", sometimes known as a "lead capture page", is the page that appears when a potential customer clicks on an advertisement or a search-engine result link. The page will usually display content that is a logical extension of the advertisement or link, and that is optimized to feature specific keywords or phrases for indexing by search engines.

Lifetime Value
The entire amount of money earned from that customer. In marketing, customer lifetime value (CLV), lifetime customer value (LCV), or lifetime value (LTV) or "customer life cycle

management" is the present value of the future cash flows attributed to the customer relationship.

Line Extension
Line extension is when a line of different new products are produced alongside an established product.

Link
A link (or 'hot link') is an instant electronic gateway (usually viewed as underlined text) from one website to another, or to different pages within the same website.

Logging On
Entering user details to access the Internet.

Market Intelligence
Market Intelligence (MI) is the information relevant to a company's markets, gathered and analyzed specifically for the purpose of accurate and confident decision-making in determining market opportunity, market penetration strategy, and market development metrics.

Maven
A "Maven" (also "Mavin") is a trusted expert in a particular field, who seeks to pass knowledge on to others.

Mb Megabyte
A unit of computer information.

Meta Tags
These are HTML tags that surround keywords and key phrases when submitting a website to a search engine.

MHz (Megahertz)
A unit of measurement of frequency. 1 megahertz = 1,000,000 hertz.

Microsoft Internet Explorer (IE)
The Internet's most popular browser.

Modem
A device that connects two computers via a telephone line.

MSN
Microsoft's online service was launched in August 1995 as a proprietary system that used the company's own development tools. Later Microsoft turned MSN into a Web-based Internet service.

Newsletter
Information, often styled in the format of a newspaper. Newsletters generally contain information that is of interest primarily to a specific group.

Network Computer
Based on Oracle's standard for low-cost Internet-ready devices, The Network Computer is a low-cost machine that connects to a TV or monitor. Local storage will be kept to a minimum as applications, such as Java, will deliver all the applications needed via the Net.

Niche
A special area of demand for a product or service. Also, a situation or activity specially suited to a person's interests, abilities, or nature.

Niche Market
A niche market is the subset of the market on which a specific product is focusing on; Therefore, the market niche defines the specific product features aimed at satisfying specific market needs, as well as the price range, production quality, and the demographics that is intending to impact.

Niche Marketing
Niche marketing is the process of finding and serving profitable market segments and designing custom-made products or services for them. For big companies those market segments are often too small in order to serve them profitably as these market segments often lack economies of scale.

Niche Market sector
A niche market is a focused, targetable portion of a market.

Offshore Business
A company that is registered in a country other than the one in which it conducts most of its business, usually for tax purposes.

Online Service Providers
Online Services Providers (OSPs) provide access to the Internet, often through a local POP. They are known as OSPs to distinguish them from the smaller ISPs. Connecting to the Internet through an OSP is an alternative to regional or local ISPs. These online companies are commercial concerns that have their own databases and information services for their own subscribers to access in addition to getting onto the Internet. There are three global online services providing Internet access: AOL (America On-Line), CompuServe and MSN (Microsoft Network). The term OSP is falling into disuse as most large ISPs now provide content etc.

Open-Ended Questions
Unstructured question in which (unlike in a multiple choice question) possible answers are not suggested, and the respondent answers it in his or her own words.

Over-Capitalization
A company is said to be over-capitalized when its total of owned and borrowed capital exceeds its fixed and current assets (i.e. when it shows accumulated losses on the assets side of the balance sheet).

Overheads
Cost or expense (such as for administration, insurance, rent, and utility charges) that (i) relates to an operation or the firm as a whole, (ii) does not become an integral part of a good or service (unlike raw material or direct labor), and (iii) cannot be applied or traced to any specific unit of output. Overheads are indirect costs.

Pareto 80/20 Ratio
The Pareto Principle (also known as 'The 80/20 Rule') states that, for many events, roughly 80% of the effects come from 20% of the causes (e.g. 80% of your sales come from 20% of your clients).

Pay Per Click (PPC)
Online advertising payment model in which payment is based solely on qualifying click-throughs. The advertiser only pays for qualifying clicks to the destination website based on a prearranged per-click rate.

POP3
Post Office Protocol Number 3 (POP3). Not a "point of presence" (POP) but a method of sending email messages.

Press Release
An announcement of an event, performance, or other newsworthy item that is issued to the press.

Price Sensitivity
A research method for establishing the range of prices that buyers are willing to pay for a product or service.

Prospect
A sales term for a 'potential customer'. A potential customer or client qualified on the basis or his or her buying authority, financial capacity, or willingness to buy.

Risk Eliminator
The *Risk Eliminator*™ system is an online market research tool used to predict the demand for products or services before launch.

RSS
RSS is the acronym used to describe the *de facto* standard for the syndication of Web content. RSS is an XML-based format and while it can be used in different ways for content distribution, its most widespread usage is in distributing news headlines on the Web.

RSS Advertising
Advertising using RSS platform to deliver it.

Search Engine
A website dedicated to helping to find information simply by typing words or phrases into a search text box.

Segmentation
Market segmentation is a marketing technique that targets a group of customers with specific characteristics, such as lifestyle.

Self-Actualization
The motive to realize all of one's potentialities. The final level of psychological development that can be achieved when all basic and mental needs are fulfilled and the "actualization" of the full personal potential takes place.

SEO (Search Engine Optimization)
The process of increasing the amount of visitors to a website by ranking higher in the search results of a search engine. SEO helps to ensure that a website is accessible to a search engine and improves the chances that the website will be found by the search engine.

Server
The central computer; making services and data available.

Social Networking
A social network is a social structure made of nodes (which are generally individuals or organizations) that are tied by one or more specific types of interdependency, such as values, visions, ideas, financial exchange, friendship, sexual relationships, kinship, dislike, conflict or trade.

Spreadsheet
A table of values arranged in rows and columns. Each value can have a predefined relationship to the other values.

Shareware

Software that can be downloaded from the Internet for a free trial period, or totally free of charge (the latter is commonly known as *Freeware*).

Shareware.com

The Internet is full of free software and www.shareware.com is the place to find it. This huge website categorizes thousands of applications and allows a search for elusive software.

Strategic Synergy

Strategic Synergy™ is the phenomena of improved performance through cooperative strategies, such as through the use of affiliate or partnership schemes.

Strategic Fit

Strategic Fit™ is the state in which the activities of an organization match the environment in which it conducts commerce. This state can be tested using the *Strategic Fit Matrix*™. For a small business owner-manager, evaluating whether or not their particular business has the correct strategic fit for Internet commerce will be the most critical judgment they must make.

Template

A document or file (e.g. website template) having a preset format, used as a starting point for a particular application so that the format does not have to be recreated each time it is used.

Unique Proposition Strategy

A company's *Unique Proposition Strategy*™ (UPS) is a combination of its Unique Selling Proposition (USP), Unique Value Proposition (UVP) and Unique Tactical Plan (UTP).

Unique Tactical Plan (UTP)

The tactics, logistics and strategy used to employ a company's Unique Selling Proposition (USP) and Unique Value Proposition (UVP).

Unique Selling Proposition (USP)
The Unique Selling Proposition (also Unique Selling Point) is a marketing concept, which states that marketing campaigns should make unique propositions to the customer to convince them to switch brands.

Unique Value Proposition (UVP)
A customer Value Proposition consists of the sum total of benefits which a vendor promises that a customer will receive in return for the customer's associated payment (or other value-transfer).

Upload
To transfer information from one computer to another directly over the Internet.

Upgrade
To make an improvement to your current system; usually changing old software or hardware for up-to-date versions.

URL
The Universal Resource Locator is the command that points to the Web address. This facility means users don't have to remember lengthy and unmemorable IP addresses.

Vanguard
The foremost or leading position in a trend or movement, such as the first company to enter a new market.

Vendor
A manufacturer, producer, or seller.

Viral marketing
Marketing phenomenon that facilitates and encourages people to pass along a marketing message. Similar to word-of-mouth marketing, viral marketing depends on a high pass-along rate from person to person.

Visitor
'Visitors' are individuals accessing a website via the Internet. 'Unique visitors' defines the number of individual visitors who access a website during the time period of the report. A unique visitor is counted only once even if they access the website more than once during the time period of the report.

Word-of-Mouth
Word-of-mouth marketing is based on customers talking to each other about a product or service, rather than formalized, structured, paid-for advertising. Its success depends on positive feedback and a high pass-along rate from person to person.

Web Hosting
The act of publishing a website.

Website
A collection of documents or information published on the World Wide Web.

Yahoo!
Yahoo! (www.yahoo.com) is a giant directory to thousands of websites and one of the most popular websites on the Internet.

You'll Make $ERIOUS
MONEY Online!

Index

Fortune Cookie